GOLF
Past 50

AGELESS ATHLETE SERIES

GOLF
Past 50

David Chmiel
Editor in Chief, *Senior Golfer*

Kevin Morris, EdD
Managing Editor/Features, *Senior Golfer*

Human Kinetics

Library of Congress Cataloging-in-Publication Data

Chmiel, David, 1961-
    Golf past 50 / David Chmiel, Kevin Morris.
       p. cm. -- (Ageless athlete series)
    Includes index.
    ISBN 0-7360-0211-1
    1. Golf for the aged. I. Title: Golf past 50. II. Morris, Kevin (Kevin B.) III. Title. IV.
Series.

    GV966.5 .C46 2001
    796.352'084'6--dc21

                                           00-057542
                                              CIP

ISBN: 0-7360-0211-1

Acquisitions Editor: Martin Barnard; **Managing Editor:** Cynthia McEntire; **Assistant Editor:** Kim Thoren; **Copyeditor:** Robert Replinger; **Indexer:** Daniel A. Connolly; **Permission Manager:** Cheri Banks; **Graphic Designer:** Robert Reuther; **Graphic Artist:** Francine Hamerski; **Photo Manager:** Clark Brooks; **Cover Designer:** Keith Blomberg; **Photographer (cover):** © Michael Zito/SportsChrome USA; **Photographer (interior):** Tom Roberts unless otherwise noted; **Printer:** Versa Press

Human Kinetics books are available at special discounts for bulk purchase. Special editions or book excerpts can also be created to specification. For details, contact the Special Sales Manager at Human Kinetics.

Printed in the United States of America

10 9 8 7 6 5 4 3 2 1

Human Kinetics
Web site: www.humankinetics.com

United States: Human Kinetics
P.O. Box 5076
Champaign, IL 61825-5076
800-747-4457
e-mail: humank@hkusa.com

Canada: Human Kinetics
475 Devonshire Road Unit 100
Windsor, ON N8Y 2L5
800-465-7301 (in Canada only)
e-mail: hkcan@mnsi.net

Europe: Human Kinetics, P.O. Box IW14
Leeds LS16 6TR, United Kingdom
+44 (0) 113 278 1708
e-mail: humank@hkeurope.com

Australia: Human Kinetics
57A Price Avenue
Lower Mitcham, South Australia 5062
08 8277 1555
e-mail: liahka@senet.com.au

New Zealand: Human Kinetics
P.O. Box 105-231, Auckland Central
09-309-189
e-mail: hkp@ihug.co.nz

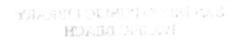

*To Paula, Zachary,and the rest of my family
who make every day fun and worthwhile.*

—David Chmiel

For Hazel Morris (1908-1997)

—Kevin Morris

Contents

Preface

You've finally gotten what you wanted—access to some of that disposable income you were shrewd enough to hide from the children and a greenside dream house in a spot that rarely gets cold. You've found a young and eager business partner who doesn't mind your vacation jaunts, and those kids haven't moved back into the house—yet. It looks like you've finally gotten the breaks you've been waiting so long for. Now it's your time to play more golf than you've played in the last 20 years.

Mark Twain once said that youth is wasted on the young, but you may be amending that to read, "Retirement is wasted on the old." As you gear up for more time on the fairways than in the boardroom, you're concerned that your new-found freedom might come with a price—a limit on energy and enthusiasm as well as some deterioration of athletic skills over the years. You're faced with a sense of melancholy. You lament the 20 yards off the tee that you can't seem to reclaim. You deplore the loss of accuracy with those long irons, the precision that once allowed you to birdie the tough par-fours or make remarkable recovery shots from the deep rough. Maybe the joy you once had for slinging the clubs over your shoulder and walking the course is waning, weakened by a lack of stamina that saps your strength by the 14th hole.

And although those concerns may be appropriate, they are neither a fait accompli nor irreversible. Look around you. Age is not a life sentence—it's a life's work. And as you look around, take time to notice that people your age and much older are leading healthier, more productive lives than those of any generation before. If you want to play better, live longer, and enjoy those 50-and-over years, you must carry the same commitment you took with you to work every day—a responsibility to climb that corporate ladder to provide for your family, obtain financial freedom, and secure your well-being. It worked in your business life; is it unreasonable to think that you can apply that determination to rededicating yourself to your golf game?

Of course, there's another reason why you need to find your way to better health and longevity in the game. The American population is graying. The baby boomer generation is not simply the concoction of some publicist looking for the latest next big thing. It is a real phenomenon. According to statistics, someone in this country will turn 50 every seven seconds through the year 2007. Consequently, the nation will soon have more 50-and-over residents than ever before. And certainly we have strength in numbers, because today's 50-and-overs look and feel better than their parents ever did at that age. Today's older adults are more aware of the importance that diet, exercise, and generally healthy lifestyles hold for improved quality of life—especially if it means beating the kids and grandkids from tee to green.

The evolution of the Senior PGA Tour is proof that turning 50 does nothing to hurt your golf game. Since the tour's inception in 1980, players from Arnold Palmer and Gary Player to Hale Irwin and Gil Morgan have shown that there is life after 50 on the fairways and greens. Add to that 58-year-old Jack Nicklaus's sixth-place finish in the 1998 Masters and 48-year-old Tom Watson's victory over the flatbellies at the PGA Tour's '98 Mastercard Colonial and you should recognize your potential.

Golf Past 50 will provide helpful hints on how equipment manufacturers are using the latest breakthroughs in technology to build clubs that will help players 50 and over hit it longer while keeping it in the fairway as well as anecdotes and case studies on how Senior PGA Tour players prepared for life on the "mulligan" tour. Success in your golf game as you approach, or have passed, 50 is in your hands. *Golf Past 50* will provide the right start.

Photo Credits

Introduction

The Best Golf Lies Ahead

It seems as though you turned 19 two weeks ago, when your big concerns centered around buying some beer to impress your date and studying for that History 101 exam while simultaneously starting and finishing a 20-page term paper on *The Last of the Mohicans* without having read the book. That was the hard part.

The easy part was running, jumping, lifting, and swinging. No matter what sport you were playing, you could run all day, get a drink of water, and be ready to play again.

You're older now, of course, but everything is going smoothly. You've reached a simple rhythm in your life. You're firing on all cylinders. You've got a great spouse and a loving and maturing family. The career is going swimmingly. You have a full, rich life away from the office—full of friends, social events, and plenty of golf. You get away to agreeable places every couple of months, tying in a couple business-golf trips throughout the year. Life is good.

Then you step into the house after work one Friday and the next thing you know you're in the middle of a surprise party. People are screaming into your unsuspecting face, slapping you on the back, and making you open boxes of trusses, ginkoba, eca, eca, eca-something and joking that really, no kidding, you look great.

You have no idea what hit you until you see that cake on the dining room table.

Fifty. Half a century. The big five-oh. Brother, what am I going to do now? Most days, you're fine with this treacherous turn of events. You've come to grips with the concept that life is a marathon, not a sprint. But all those candles . . .

Actually, you know darn well that things are getting even better. You've reached a point in your life where you've made your way up the corporate ladder or used your entrepreneurial skills to build a ladder of your own.

Despite mortgage payments, braces, tuition bills, and that little lakeside cabin the kids couldn't live without, you've managed to hide enough money from those kids to guarantee a comfortable future. They're either living on their own or on their way out of the house—or at least have yet to return—and you're looking at the opportunity to scale back on the work hours and concentrate on enjoying more free time. You have committed to spending more time relaxing and getting back into those pursuits that time pressure squeezed out as you balanced work and family.

Heck, I'm golden. This is nothing. I even blew out those candles in one clean shot. But man, there sure were a lot of them . . .

Listen, just give it a break. Let those thoughts go in and out of your head. Look at yourself. You've never been more active— you may be inline skating with your children, biking with your loved ones, walking or running every morning before work or every night after dinner. You're watching your diet and even sneaking in those lunchtime workouts. You may have started on this regimen knowing what lay ahead, but it's gotten you to the point where you are feeling better than you have in years.

So cut yourself a bit of slack. Although some of the pressures have started to ease and you can see yourself not going into the office every day, or at least going in for just a few hours before you sneak out to play a quick 9—or a leisurely 18—*Golf Past 50* is here to tell you that you're not alone and that some of your best golf is ahead of you.

Of course, you may be one of the millions of 60-and-over golfers out there who have picked up this book to get tips on anything from how improved nutrition can boost your stamina on those last few holes to finding short-game solutions for beating those bogeys to learning from Senior PGA Tour stars that you need not sacrifice distance off the tee simply because you've reached a certain stage in your life. By now, you're comfortable in your own skin, harboring no illusion that you can buy back 10 years any more than you can summon the interest to audit a differential calculus class at the local community college. You know your golf game and are looking for an edge, to be sure, but you're not interested in trying to re-create the Tiger Woods swing, at least not without an orthopedic surgeon nearby.

This brings us to the likely reason this book has been commissioned—the baby boomers. This gang of tens of millions—the archetypal generation carrying colossal clout in their bank accounts and in the trunks of their luxury import automobiles and sports-utility vehicles—is taking all the credit and getting all the attention of the aging of America. Perhaps they should—after all, boomers represent 30 percent of the current population and 45 percent of all household heads. According to statistics from the Census Bureau, someone in the United States will turn 50 every seven seconds through the year 2007.

Somewhere after the summer of love in 1969, radical activist Abbie Hoffman said, "Never trust anyone over 30." When he said that, the median age of Americans was 28. Half the population was older than 28, and the other half was younger than 28. By the year 2020, the median age will be 39. In 1990, approximately 37,000 people celebrated their 100th—or older—birthdays. By 2010, 131,000 people will be 100 or older.

Sobering numbers indeed. And although these numbers reflect the "pig in the python" analogy so often linked to the baby boomers' effect on the world around them, what about now and that intimate relative, five years from now?

It's as simple as this—there's been much talk about the graying of America because numbers simply can't reflect the impact of one generation without trying to squeeze it into a compartmentalized unit.

As a result, the argument goes, the median age is increasing, which must mean that we've got a lot of older people around. Well, although that may be technically accurate, it's not entirely representative because the 50-and-over population has never been, to borrow from Ben Franklin, healthier, wealthier, or wiser. It can be easily argued that your generation is more concerned with living better longer and is succeeding. And although you realize that it's important to beat demons such as obesity, high cholesterol, high blood pressure, and the rest of those nasty maladies, you're doing it not just to live longer, but to really live—enjoying children and grandchildren, traveling, and taking full advantage of an active lifestyle.

That brings us to your golf game. You've been playing golf for a long time, long enough to have expectations of it, long enough to start worrying about what's going to happen to your game as you get set for match play with Father Time. We are here to tell you that you have no reason to believe that your game is suddenly going to disappear—provided you're willing to take preventative steps to keep you, and it, healthy.

Combine societal emphasis on wellness and quality-of-life issues such as improved cardiovascular health, low-fat diets, and trimmer waistlines with the commitment of the golf industry to improved instruction and technologically advanced equipment and you'll agree that there's never been a better time to make an effort to improve your golf game.

Playing well and playing well longer are reasonable and reachable goals, provided you're prepared to match your expectations with the work it will take to reach them. A commitment to improved fitness isn't a guaranteed ticket to shaving strokes off your handicap. Improving stamina and maintaining or restoring supple muscle tissue are vital to wellness and longevity, but they'll help your golf swing only if you spend the time to hone it the way you do your body. Just as you need to make accommodations in worst-case scenarios—swinging around a big stomach or shortening a swing to avoid overtaxing a bad shoulder or wrist—you must also work hard on the practice range to take advantage of improved flexibility.

Telling those of you who have picked up this book that it's important to work on yourself and your game is like preaching to the converted. You either are prepared to do something or are in the process of reclaiming your body or your golf game. Otherwise, you wouldn't be reading this. And honestly, although we are gearing what you will see over the next nine chapters for golfers 50 and over, the message is the same for any golfer. Don't let yourself get into a spot that prevents you from getting the most from the game you love so dearly. We all want to play better. Each of us wants to walk off the golf course feeling that our game wasn't hindered by lack of conditioning, by not spending enough time on the practice range, by not eating right, by not playing the proper equipment, or by not thinking our way around the course.

We can blame deficiencies on added years or added pounds. But let's be clear about it. The golf ball doesn't know the age of the person who hit it, the club doesn't know the age of the person swinging it, and the scorecard doesn't know the age of the hand that just wrote in four pars in a row. That said, let's also be clear that certain things we once possessed won't be coming back. But that doesn't mean that those concessions are going to cost us the enjoyment of the game or the ability to score as well as we have in the past. Those childhood rounds that included four birdies and five double-bogeys can give way to the round of a mature golfer who thinks his or her way around the course and plays an improved short game to produce one birdie, six pars, and two bogeys. Remember what generations of short, straight hitters have said quietly to themselves as they watched overswinging knuckleheads look for ways to punch out of trouble: "The woods are full of long hitters."

You've shown interest in improving. *Golf Past 50* will give you everything you need to take you from theory to practice. Read on with commitment to improve. Work on your diet and forge a repeatable swing that you can depend on. Hone the shotsaving skills—physical and mental—that will have you playing better golf than you imagined possible. Do all this and you may secure the ultimate revenge, winning those $5 Nassaus from the kids who underestimate the guy with graying temples and the gal with silver locks.

1

Checking Your Swing

The genius of a good swing is in the ability to consistently put the clubface squarely on the ball. The golf swing is an incredibly complex motion. Great players address the ball with confidence, knowing they have a swing they can repeat as often as they need to. They know that as long as the fundamentals are in place, the details will take care of themselves.

Sure, as we age, it becomes harder to retain some physical skills. But if you can improve your technique, adjust your strategic approach, and work hard to take care of yourself as your body changes, you'll continue to enjoy the game instead of cursing the aging process and growing frustrated on the course. Although it's natural to lose some strength and flexibility, the remarkable thing about golf is that you can improve most aspects of your game as you age. Players on the Senior PGA Tour prove that every week. Hale Irwin, for example, who had a remarkable career, felt he played his best golf when he turned 50.

Let's assume you're an enthusiastic amateur player. In terms of your overall life and the importance of golf, let's put your game into perspective:

- Make your health your first priority. Let's ensure that your swing isn't putting unnecessary stress on your body and putting your future health or posture at risk.
- Assess the strengths of your game. Let's build on your strengths and try to eliminate your weaknesses.
- Try to stay fit and strong but also learn to accept the natural loss of physical power. The key is to focus on being a smarter player.

This chapter deals with the fundamentals of the swing—some swing checks that will remind you of the swing's essential components and guide you in adapting your swing as you age. Many schools of thought offer ideas about how a player should adapt his or her swing over time. A great deal of contradictory information is available, so it's difficult to know what will work for you. The bottom line is that everyone has a different swing and body type. Golden rules don't exist.

You probably started learning the game many years ago, and it may have been years since you've had a lesson. Regardless, the most effective way to analyze your game and build a swing is to return to ground zero—the swing essentials.

Here are five swing fundamentals to consider for your health and the future of your game.

The Grip

A good grip will not only help you maximize accuracy and power but also help you swing comfortably and painlessly. As top players move to senior ranks, many change their grips to maintain athleticism in their swings and avoid injuries. Every player's goal is to have power and control, but few of us have the strength and suppleness that we did at age 25. Here are a few ideas you should consider for your grip.

a weak grip

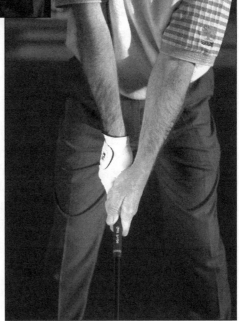

b normal grip

(continued)

How you grip the club will influence the power of your swing.

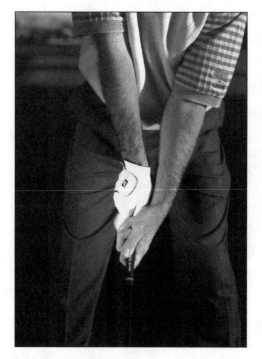

c   strong grip

Hand Position

Many senior players use a stronger grip, with the Vs in their hands positioned just slightly farther around the shaft to the right (for right-handers), away from the target. If you move your hands just a quarter of an inch, your entire setup will feel markedly different. This grip should help you rotate your torso easily and get your weight and head behind the ball at impact, thus generating more power. This doesn't work for everyone, so experiment and ask a teaching professional to help you.

You will also find that a stronger grip will force you to swing on a flatter inside-outside swing plane, which may also eliminate any slice problems.

Perfect position at impact.

GET A GRIP

Hale Irwin

Proper hand and arm position can help you avoid two of the more common mistakes I see, particularly in people playing long irons—the "fire and fall back" and "the cast out."

We could do a whole book on the proper grip, but here are the basics. Your grip only needs to be tight enough to prevent the club from flying out of your hands; any tighter and you'll restrict your arm movement. A sign that you're holding the club too tightly is in the coloration of your fingertips—bright red and white blotches are trouble. Loosen your grip until skin color is relatively uniform.

Arm position can also affect your grip. As I mentioned earlier, make sure your rear shoulder (my right) is slightly lower to the ground and that your rear arm (my right) is a tad closer to your body than is your front (my left) arm. Note in the photo, taken from behind me, that you can see a little bit of my left arm in front of my right arm. That's a good position. Remember that tension often promotes a bad or tight grip. Always make sure you feel loose before you begin the swing.

Grip Down

Although you may be reluctant to crouch over the ball any farther, gripping the club slightly farther down the shaft may help you develop feel and control of the clubhead. You may lose a few yards with each club, but the extra control will compensate for that. Crouching may cause you to bend your knees more than usual, which may take some pressure off your back. Again, just the slightest shift will feel radically different, so experiment with this concept. You may find it useful only for some situations or clubs.

You may develop control by gripping the club farther down the shaft.

Close Hands, Constant Pressure

Your hands should work together, with the palms of your hands parallel to each other throughout your swing. The three most common grips are the baseball, or ten-fingered, grip; the interlocking, with your left index finger sliding between the ring finger and small finger of your right hand; and the overlapping, with the left index finger resting on top of your right ring finger and small finger.

How tightly do you grip the club? Top players generally suggest that grip pressure should be firm but not tight, tightening just before and during impact. If you can see the grip between your fingers, your hands and fingers are not working as closely together as they could. A tight bond between your fingers ensures that your hands work as a unit. Be sure, though, that your grip isn't restricting your backswing.

Flat Sole

Is the sole of your club lying flat on the ground at address? As players age, they tend to crouch over the ball, keeping their hands low with the toe of the club off the ground.

You can use the sole of the club to determine a good posture and setup. If the angle of your shaft is correct, the entire sole will rest flat on the grass. The resulting shaft angle will help you set your hands and align your posture accordingly. If only the heel of the club is resting on the ground, it's likely that you're crouched over the ball too much, with your hands too low to the ground. Attention to the sole of the club will help you retain your spine angle and provide the maximum opportunity to return the clubface to the ball in a square position.

Conversely, if the heel is not touching the ground, the shaft may be too upright. When the sole of the club is flat, you're more likely to make solid contact if you return the club to the same position at impact.

The interlocking grip is one of three common choices.

The sole of the club will be flat on the grass if your angle and alignment
are correct.

If your hands are too low to the ground, the sole of the club will not lie flat.

Stance and Alignment

The alignment of your body to the target is crucial to consistent shotmaking. It is important to find a routine that allows you to align yourself for each shot. From a health point of view, good alignment also takes stress away from your spine.

A Stress-Free Swing

The goal with your stance is to set yourself into a relaxed position—one that allows you to turn with balance and control—and ultimately make solid, square contact with the ball. If your stance is relaxed, you should be able to make a tension-free, safe swing without putting too much pressure on your back.

If you want to remove some stress from your back, try turning your front foot outward, slightly toward the target. This will help you complete your follow-through and rotate your body more easily.

The biggest challenge in aligning the clubface and your body with the target is eliminating the small, instinctive position adjustments just before making a swing. Without realizing it, many players change their posture and alignment as they address the ball, and it's easy to develop some disastrous habits. Let a teaching professional help you develop a routine for getting and staying in position as you hit a shot.

If your shoulders move just slightly at address, you may become slightly closed or open to the target. And if you don't feel confident about your address position, it's unlikely you'll be able to swing with confidence. Take the time to make sure you're aligned and comfortable. On the range, you have probably seen players lay clubs on the ground, one on the target line and another parallel with it near the tops of the toes (see photo on page 14). This drill helps you sustain a position that's square to your target.

Take stress off your back! Turn your front foot slightly toward your target.

Senior PGA Tour player Tom Wargo uses this drill to keep his swing on target.

Have someone watch you to check the alignment of your shoulders and feet. Another effective drill is to place a club across your knees in the address position and see where the club shaft is pointing. Lee Trevino (see photo) is an example of a player who uses an unorthodox stance, but then he also has incredible talent. His body is not squarely aligned to the target at address, but he still manages to get the clubface square at impact. Others prefer a closed stance because it allows them to get to the top of their swings with ease, placing less stress on the torso.

Lee Trevino's unorthodox style works, but he's also very talented.

SETUP AND ALIGNMENT

Jim Colbert

At least 90 percent of the amateurs I play with aim the ball 30 yards into the right woods. They hit it there and then wonder why. The problem is that they look at the ball, not the target, when they place their feet. This six-step procedure for setting up correctly will immediately improve your shots, regardless of what swing faults you might have.

1. While looking at the target, with your body open to the target, place your right foot in the approximate position it will be when you hit the shot, perpendicular to the target line. At this stage, just your left hand is on the club.

2. Pick up the club and put your right hand snugly in place (photo a). At the same time, plug your left arm softly into your body, resting it gently against the left side of your chest.

3. Keeping your back straight, bend slightly at the knees, set the clubface behind the ball, and aim it at the target. Your body is still in an open position, and you're looking at the target.

4. Place your left foot in position, with your eyes still on the target (photo b). If you look down and don't keep the target in view, your body is likely to become closed and you'll end up aiming to the right.

5. Adjust the right foot, moving it into its final position. At this point you can move the foot so your stance is square, open, or closed, depending on the type of shot you're planning to play. Keep your eyes on the target.

6. Set your club squarely behind the ball and hit it.

a

b

Your ball position is also crucial to your setup. The type of club should determine how far forward the ball should be in your stance. For longer clubs, the ball should be in line with the inside heel of your front foot, but move the ball further toward your back foot as the clubs get shorter. If the ball is too far forward in your stance, you will have to reach for the ball and will close the face of the club at impact. If the ball is too far back, you'll be hitting down on the ball with the clubface open.

Spine Angle, Posture, and Swing Plane

Your address position should also establish an angle for your spine. In turn, your spine angle will determine your swing plane. If you can maintain a constant spine angle throughout your swing, the club will stay on a constant plane, simplifying your swing and increasing its consistency. If your spine angle changes during a swing, the club moves off its plane. This deviation complicates the path of the club back to the ball and increases stress on your back. You should determine the address position that minimizes stress on your body and allows you to get the clubface onto the ball.

If you're not conscious of your spine angle, you will need to learn to swing with what seems like a stiff spine. Rather than crouching over the ball with a bent spine, bend from the hips, flex your knees, and keep your spine straight and fairly upright. You will feel pressure in your lower back, but you will then swing the club around your body with your shoulders level.

Keep your spine upright by bending from the hips and flexing your knees.

THE BACKSWING AND SWING PLANE

David Graham

A common misconception is that the golf swing is vertical. It's not. The club must swing in a tilted circle around your body as various parts of your body turn. The turn of your body is crucial, especially with a driver. When you hit your driver, the longest club in your bag, you're standing farthest from the ball. You must take a full turn with your shoulders—90 degrees or as far as you can turn them—so that the club can swing inside the target line or around your body on the backswing. The trend toward 45- and 46-inch drivers may be the best thing that ever happened to the amateur player because these longer drivers force you to stand farther from the ball and encourage a slightly flatter plane.

The Backswing

A comfortable backswing becomes more difficult as we age simply because we lose natural flexibility and it becomes more difficult to get into an athletic position at the top of the swing. You can use several methods to maximize the rotation of your body so that you get into a good backswing position.

First, the rotation of your hips and trunk should drive the rotation of your backswing. As golfers age, they tend to lift their arms during a backswing rather than swinging the club *around* their bodies. If your hips rotate, your arms and shoulders must rotate with them.

Rotate your hips to drive your backswing.

THE BACKSWING

Bob Murphy

The key to a good backswing, which, of course, is the key to a good forward swing, is to swing your arms and the club back high and wide. I feel that I'm pushing with my left shoulder, but obviously the hands and arms are swinging, too. I can only describe it by saying that if I took a rod and placed it between my left shoulder and the clubface, the shoulder would push the clubface back.

If you are well-balanced at address, you will find it easier to rotate your body.

Weight Transfer and Balance

The transfer of your body weight first to your back leg and then to your front leg generates most of the power in your swing. If you shift your weight too far in either direction, however, you will find it difficult to maintain your balance. On your backswing, for example, your weight should move to the inside of your right foot, not the outside. If your weight moves to the outside of your foot, you're forced to change your swing plane simply to stay balanced.

At the end of your follow-through, you should raise your right heel to allow your body to turn and face the target, with your weight on the outside of your front foot. Despite the shift in weight, your body should always remain level. Your upper body should remain in essentially the same position throughout the swing. As you follow through, most of your weight should end up on your front leg, with your torso pointing toward the target. Raising the heel of your front foot slightly off the ground as you turn will increase the flexibility and rotation of your backswing.

Weight shift on backswing.

Over-swinging will force you to be off balance.

Correct weight transfer at follow-through.

BALANCE

Larry Nelson

Sometimes in practice sessions when I feel my balance slipping a little during my backswing, I'll take the club back to the top and stop it. I'll check the position of my hands and arms, and I'll make adjustments until I feel I'm in good balance on my right side. I'll start down from there. You just swing the club to the top, pause until you feel that you're set properly in good balance on your right side, and then swing through the ball. Doing this will help you identify the feeling you should have at the top when you're on the course.

Step Drill

The best way to practice a balanced weight shift is to step with your right leg over your left after you make contact. As you near the end of your follow-through, just take a step with your right foot over your left (see photos). You won't be able to pick up your right foot unless all your weight has transferred to the left side.

AVOID THE REVERSE PIVOT

Gil Morgan

The problem in golf is that we don't move our feet as we do in other sports. If we move our feet, we often create a large power leak from the swing, the reverse pivot (photo). Instead of shifting the weight to the back foot, a player moves more of it to the front foot. This often results from an attempt to keep the head still. If you have your weight on the front foot at the top of the backswing, the only place it can go is to the back foot on the forward swing. Obviously, this kind of swing diminishes clubhead speed and power.

DOWNSWING AND FOLLOW-THROUGH

Al Geiberger

Once you have swung back as far as your body allows, you can correctly start the forward swing in several ways. I like to think first of planting my left heel. Doing this starts a chain reaction that turns the left hip. Turning the hips to the target is critical in making a good finish. As you're making that first move down with your lower body, let your arms drop from the top of your swing. By just letting gravity pull them down, you won't spin your shoulders. Your upper body will drop in behind your left leg, and your club will settle on the correct plane. Then everything else just kicks in.

Many golfers execute a lazy follow-through. They don't turn their hips actively through impact. Instead of turning to point the midsection directly at the target, they finish with the hips turned only partially toward it. Most of the weight remains on the back foot. To put a little more power in your downswing, simply think of moving that left hip farther around on the follow-through. Turn your midsection more aggressively and finish with all your weight on your front foot.

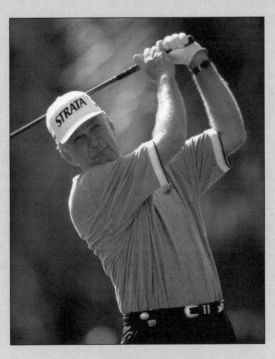

Tempo

If you're losing distance as you age, you're losing flexibility and your ability to generate clubhead speed—it's as simple as that. Strength and flexibility training will help you retain some of your power, but the average person loses a considerable amount of hand speed.

Other factors, however, can help you sustain your game and compensate for your loss of power. Shifting your focus toward your tempo and rhythm, for example, may help you considerably. Why is tempo so important? All great players swing with a pace that allows them to position their bodies to make solid contact with the ball. All have different swing speeds, but each has found a rhythm that affords control of the swing by using rhythm and balance.

Most amateurs simply swing more quickly than their technique and hand-eye coordination allow. Their swings aren't grooved well enough or technically advanced enough to retain their direction and shape or allow for the pace of their movement. Everyone has a natural swing speed. The important point is to accelerate your swing into the ball. If you decelerate into impact position, it is likely that you have accelerated at the top of your swing as you're beginning your downswing. A slower backswing will help in two ways: it will allow you to get into a consistent position at the top of your swing and allow you to accelerate the turn of your body as your downswing gains momentum. If your swing loses speed as it approaches the ball, it's likely that your body and arms will be out of position for a clean hit of the ball. A "heavy" shot often results.

Beyond changing the pace of your backswing, it's unlikely you'll be able to change your overall swing speed drastically from its natural pace. Quick swingers always have trouble gearing down their momentum, just as slow swingers have trouble increasing their natural arm speed. During practice, swing at different speeds to discover a rhythm that is effective for you. Remember that accelerating into the ball is crucial.

TEMPO

Hale Irwin

The key to good tempo is good alignment and posture—where you are aimed, how your body is aligned to that aiming point, and how you stand up to the ball. All of that leads to the proper start of your swing.

Lay a club on the ground on the practice tee parallel to your target line. Then align your feet, knees, and hips square to that club. I want to feel that my shoulders are slightly open or turned to the left of the target, mainly because my right hand is below the left on the club.

Assume an athletic position. Flex your knees slightly, as if you were ready to run, jump, or dance.

Your should feel controlled tension, ready to hit the ball with maximum efficiency. Golf is a game of gentle firmness. If you have taken the correct position at the start, just take the club back to the top and return it to where it started.

You can learn almost everything I've discussed by simply hitting balls with your feet together, or at least with a very narrow stance. I do it with any club, including the driver. If you swing too hard, especially from the top, you'll fall over. This drill makes you stay steady over the ball through the hitting area. You can't lunge at it and move your center of mass off the ball. The drill requires you to swing your arms around your trunk instead of trying to muscle the ball. It offers a simple way to find your probable swing pace and tempo and helps you determine your ideal swing plane because you'll be swinging more naturally.

Another good practice-tee drill is to swing at 50 percent of your capacity. Try to hit your driver 100 or 150 yards. You'll probably find that it goes farther than that because you're making solid contact.

The Impact Position

The preceding points are irrelevant if you can't get yourself into a good position at impact. As Johnny Miller always says, "There is only one inch that's important in golf—a half inch before impact and a half inch after impact." Look at your swing in a mirror and ask yourself the following questions:

- Where are my hands at impact? Are they too far ahead of or behind the clubface?
- Is the clubface square to the target at impact?
- Where is my body weight at impact? Is it still on my back foot?

CONTROL AND ACCURACY

Hale Irwin

Another good way to control your game is to swing at 75 percent, especially with your irons. Instead of swinging the club back to parallel or close to it at the top, feel like you're making a three-quarter backswing. Grip down on the handle a couple of inches and just make a compact little swing.

When you swing, you should always feel as though you have a little bit left, that you have an untapped reserve.

In this chapter we've tried to stress the importance of knowing your game—assessing your strengths and eliminating your weaknesses. That's easier said than done, of course, but taking those steps will simplify your game. You can accomplish a lot before you actually swing the club, particularly gripping the club correctly and aligning yourself with the target. With these fundamentals in place, you can concentrate on developing the tempo of your swing.

chapter 2

Getting Some Extra Distance

Players who tell you that they don't care about getting more distance off the tee are either lying or have infallible short games. If you don't believe it, look around. Spend a few hours in the grill room and listen to players lamenting their deficiencies off the tee and telling of how they hear those two irritating words—"you're away"—echo in their ears every time they reach the spot where their drives stopped rolling. Go to the pro shop and watch players ogle the latest in distance-promising equipment, lost in titanium daydreams of the day they will finally start letting that big dog bark. Hang out at the driving range and do a little research—how many players are working on their bump-and-run games or 30-yard lob wedges and how many are getting blisters as they grip and rip driver after driver?

Now there is nothing wrong with getting more yards—we'd all rather hit 7-irons than 3-irons into the green. But if we're going to get serious about this universal problem, we have to be honest with ourselves and our games. When we meet someone new at a cocktail party and find out that he or she plays golf, we go right at it. What's your handicap? What's your favorite course? How often do you get to play? And finally, how far do you knock it off the tee? Then comes the big lie.

"Oh, I send it out there about (supply your own myth) yards with a nice, controlled little draw." OK, give yourself one last pat on the back right now—mostly for keeping a straight face all these years—because it's time to put the big lie to rest for good. You did hit it that far once—from an elevated tee, with a hurricane at your back, and with the added distance only a cart path can provide. But you never offer an average distance, and that last time you were on the left side of the fairway it was to give someone a ruling on casual water.

Now that we have the chest-puffing hyperbole out of the way, it's time to fix the problem. Remember the gist of all those self-help books you bought in the '70s that now prop up the wobbly legs of the rec-room couch? The first step to solving a problem is admitting that you have one. OK, let's get it out of the way. Repeat after me, "I was never a terribly long hitter, and now that my backswing seems shorter than a Mike Tyson fight, I'm having trouble getting that ball into the right spot in the fairway."

Providing that you said it—and meant it—the tough part is over. At *Senior Golfer* magazine, we've had the luxury of talking with the game's greats and those who teach them as they head for professional golf's ultimate mulligan, the Senior PGA Tour. Many of these stars have had to make adjustments to get their games, and themselves, in shape for the senior tour. In other chapters, we share the secrets from the fitness, health-care, and wellness professionals who've worked on those players. Reclaiming the body you used to have is undeniably important, but the swing is also critical.

We'll provide the following full-swing insights that we've gleaned from players and teachers over the years, but we'll do so in a way that doesn't promote a single swing that you must adapt to or fail. As most of these famous players know, especially the ones who've built the unique or quirky swings the announcers so frequently discuss, the golf swing is an individual movement that can be successful as long as the golfer applies certain fundamental principles. We'll talk about important factors such as coil, clubhead speed, weight transfer, and a square clubface at impact. We'll break the full swing into three pieces—setup, backswing, and downswing.

But before we do that, pay attention to the words of Bob Toski, former tour player and one of the greatest teachers the

Do your hands naturally hang parallel to your hips or do they turn slightly?

game has known. "To play golf well, you need to play it with effortless power, not with powerless effort. Most amateurs play the game too violently, thinking they need to 'power' the ball around the course. Look at me. I'm 73 years old, weigh 130 pounds, and still hit the ball 250 yards with a swing that looks effortless. Most golfers have not developed the sense of feel in their hands that good golf requires. They need to direct the swing with the hands, arms, and shoulders, while that action is supported by the rest of the body. Once amateurs learn to do this rather than muscle the ball with their bodies, they see that the swing is not all that difficult."

With those words in mind, it is also wise to remember the mantra of the late Harvey Penick—"You can't have a good swing if you've got a bad grip." Your grip should be fairly neutral, neither too strong (left hand rotated so far on the club that you can read the logo on the back of your glove) nor too weak (making it possible to see three knuckles on your right hand). Review chapter 1 (page 1) for more information on a proper grip. That said, the best way to find a comfortable grip is to let your hands hang at your sides. Look at whether your palms hang parallel to your hips or are turned slightly; this will prove your natural tendencies and provide a clue for placing your hands on the club.

Now that we've set our grip and begun the full-swing lesson, avoid what can often be a big problem when getting help. You're here (or on the lesson tee) for help, so don't try to impress anyone with what you know or what you can do with 100 percent concentration and the proper alignment of the planets. Go into these lessons with an open mind, willing to accept that you have been struggling. Let the clues on these pages or the wisdom of your golf professional help you reclaim some lost yards off the tee.

The Setup

As we all know, hitting a golf ball is one of the most difficult athletic endeavors because the ball just sits there waiting for you to hit it. As we go through our preswing rituals of getting ready to hit the ball, we invariably become tighter and tighter during the preparation to act instead of reacting as we do in most sports we've played. For this simple reason, the setup is the launching pad for the rest of the swing.

Proper posture, of course, is vital. And although you must put together many pieces to ensure the right positioning of the body, it can't be stressed strongly enough that you are assuming an athletic position, not unlike a shortstop or third baseman in baseball. As you take this position, you must pay attention to each facet to ensure a solid foundation to your swing.

- Grip the club lightly. You know that old saw, "Grip the club as you would a wounded bird. Hold it too tight and you crush it, too loose and it flies away." New saws become old saws because they work. Trust us, if you start with tension in the grip, you will create tension throughout your body and your swing will suffer.

- Keep your feet shoulder-width apart.

- Keep your back shoulder slightly lower than your forward shoulder.

- Bend your knees slightly and bend forward from the hips, keeping your weight equally distributed on the balls of your feet. About 60 percent of your weight should be on your back foot.

- From this athletic position, and without a club, let your arms hang naturally in front of you. This will provide the sense of how far your hands should be from your body when you address the ball with a club in your hands.

- Positioning the golf ball off your left heel will help you sweep the ball off the tee at impact.

From this position, you're now ready to make a solid move away from the golf ball. Larry Nelson, one of the longer hitters on the senior tour, stresses the need to concentrate on using the proper setup as the springboard to a balanced swing. "If you start your swing in a balanced position and make the proper moves to complete your backswing, you will find it easier to arrive at a balanced position at the top of your swing," he says. "Returning to the ball in proper balance from this position is made easy with a few simple moves. Good shots are the result of proper balance at impact."

Note how far away from your body your hands naturally fall.

To continue the baseball analogy and to guarantee that you don't start sneaking those feet too close together, remember those glory days when you were knocking home runs over the fence. As you waited for the pitcher to deliver the ball, you had your feet spread and ready to attack. In fact, hall-of-fame golfer and broadcaster Johnny Miller recently suggested that swinging a baseball bat might not be a bad idea as a stepping-stone for more power. He based his conclusion on playing golf with Michael Jordan before and after Jordan played minor-league baseball, saying that Jordan added about 20 yards in driving distance as a result of a rigorous schedule of swinging the baseball bat.

Now, this is not necessarily an endorsement of Miller's theory, but his message shouldn't be ignored, either. The muscles used for swinging a bat for power can help you generate a little heat off the tee. This doesn't mean that you have to muscle some teenage boys out of the local batting cages on a Saturday night, but it couldn't hurt to take a bat into the backyard and—provided that you've loosened up first—take a series of cuts and see if perhaps it can't be of some benefit.

Now that we're poised and ready for action, let's take the next step.

The Backswing

The key to improving or maintaining power comes from the confluence of clubhead speed and square contact, and although we'll discuss impact later in this chapter, the way to guarantee solid contact is by starting the swing on the proper path. Without proper routing, the rest of the swing is a race against yourself to get the clubhead traveling on the right road.

The best way to start on the road to power is to build a wide swing arc. As you take the club back, one simple thought— long and low—should be all you consider. By keeping the clubhead low to the ground, your arms and the club work in concert, creating a one-piece machine that is hard to break down. Strive to keep that clubhead moving just along the grass as long as you can before you feel your body begin to coil. Let your arms guide the club along the target line as long as possible to help you stay on plane with the target line as you get to the top of your backswing.

One drill to help you work on the long, low takeaway is to place a tee, a coin, or even another ball just beyond your back foot (whatever you choose should be slightly inside your toe to promote a slightly inside swing path). Simply practice hitting the object on your way back with the club. This easy drill will allow you to build a foolproof method for keeping your swing on track and will prevent the two killer mistakes caused by faulty takeaways:

1. Most golfers pick up the club quickly and then battle the need to compensate during the rest of the swing. They inevitably wind up coming in too steep to the ball and creating the dreaded left-to-right ball flight that they can't seem to shake.

2. Players on the other side of the rough take the clubhead too far inside and then try to compensate on the way down, only to cast the club and wind up hitting a big roping hook. Grooving the simple one-piece takeaway will let you play from the short grass.

We can't stress strongly enough the importance of the proper takeaway. Working on establishing this move on your way back to the top of the swing helps you build a smooth, repeatable movement. You've heard it countless times, but it bears repeating—don't try to kill it! We aren't as flexible as we were 20 years ago, but that rarely stops us from trying to recreate the glory days. That road is fraught with peril, and it's simply not worth going back to the well so you can crush one of every 10 balls, unless you'd rather play from the deep rough or the pine trees.

Gil Morgan, John Jacobs, and even Tom Watson have solid, compact swings that generate tremendous clubhead speed and plenty of distance. What they have in common is a deliberate takeaway that helps them load up for power. Now that we have you in a good position on the way back, let's talk about shoulder turn.

We've discussed that some among us might be less flexible than we once were, but let's make sure that doesn't translate to automatic loss of distance. The deliberate takeaway allows you to build clubhead speed without rushing. Remember that

John Jacobs' takeaway is long and low.

you don't hit the ball with your backswing; you set the stage for bringing the clubhead down to the ball. So as long as you can get the club back on plane—and keep it there—you're on the right track. You should generate as much shoulder turn as possible. You don't have to get the club back as far as John Daly to get your money's worth in shoulder turn.

The next time the senior tour comes to town, watch John Jacobs and see that despite a short backswing, he gets a big shoulder turn. You can establish this yourself by turning your chest and shoulders in a tight coil against your lower body (which is the stable base around which the swing revolves). As you get to point where you can coil your chest and shoulders without straining, you should feel the tension in your lower body, especially as your weight shifts to the inside of your lower leg.

Your wrists should now be hinged, and your forward shoulder should be as close to under your chin as you can muster. You're now in a balanced position and ready to start the downswing.

The Downswing

OK, you've gotten yourself into a comfortable coil and you're ready to take action, right? Well, sort of. Although the takeaway is a smooth but aggressive move in that the arms and club become one by pulling away and up to the top of the backswing, now it's time to let gravity take hold.

You've generated all the energy you can muster at the top of the backswing, and it's just waiting to be released. And release it you must. But do just that. Remember that unless you maintain a smooth swing, you risk losing the clubhead speed you built with that perfect coil. Don't rush to start down. Instead, you should feel like a prizefighter. How many haymakers have you seen turn into knockout blows? Not many, because the big windup tips off the other fighter to what's coming and gives him time to get out of the way. In this way, you can imagine that from the top of the backswing to impact, it's more like a jab or a straight right hand from Muhammad Ali—a straight line from a compact, powerfully coiled position.

THE TAKEAWAY

Brian Barnes

The most important area of the swing, I believe, is right at the start—from the moment you draw the club away until your hands have reached hip height on the backswing. With a driver, push the clubhead straight back from the ball for at least the first 24 inches. At this point, your shoulders will begin to turn and bring the club inside the target line. Your wrists, however, should remain firm.

From the top of the coil, you transfer the energy that you've accumulated. Use your right foot to kick that forward motion into gear—this allows the lower body to release in tempo with the upper body, leading the way for the arms and club to slide into a shallow, inside slot on the way to the ball.

One infallible drill will let you judge whether you have any power leaks that you need to plug to generate more distance. Grip the club at the head and make your normal swing. Since

a

John Jacobs (a) and Larry Nelson (b) during their downswings.

the grip end of the club is whistling through the swing arc, listen carefully. If you hear your swing get loud at the top of your swing, you've wasted a lot of energy getting there and it's going to be awfully difficult to replace it on the way down. Keep swinging the club this way until you hear the loudest *whoosh* at the bottom of the swing arc. Once you get that whoosh at the bottom of the swing, you'll know that you've plugged a leaky swing and are on your way to making solid contact.

b

Balance and body rotation are the keys to solid contact.

Making Solid Contact

Now we have clubhead speed moving in the right direction, like a train steaming through a mountain pass. Notice that we didn't say an out-of-control train steaming through a mountain pass. It may be a psychological trick, but try not to use words like "hit," "strike," or "crush" at this point in the swing. Think instead about the golf swing. Think back to the most pure contact you've ever made, and you'll realize that it felt almost as though you went right through a marshmallow. It may seem like semantics, but it's an important message. You're swinging through the ball and concentrating on making contact. As we hear teachers say so often, let the club do the work. That's what that $500 stick was engineered for, right?

Seriously, with the improvements you've made in setup, backswing, and downswing, you've laid the groundwork for successful completion of the swing. You've been around enough to know that it's not brute strength—if it were, your kids would be outdriving you all the time. But now you've set the stage, and it's time to complete the process. As you move the club into the impact zone, you should feel as though your lower body is moving rotationally and laterally toward the target. Your hands, arms, and club should feel as though they're moving through the zone at the same time. Your hands and arms should not come into the impact zone ahead of the clubhead. You should feel that the centrifugal force you've generated has allowed the arms and clubhead to arrive at the ball in a straight line that almost mirrors your position at address. Although your impact position should closely approximate your address position, you can finish the swing in several ways. The senior tour is home to many unusual follow-throughs and theories that go along with them.

Gary Player aggressively makes impact during the 1998 PGA Seniors Championship.

MAXIMIZE YOUR POWER

Bob Duval

How do you drive the ball a long way? By trying not to. I know it's hard to fight the temptation, but long hitters on the PGA Tour—such as Fred Couples, Davis Love III, and my son, David—don't crank up to hit the ball. They conserve energy by keeping their wrists cocked and their shoulders back well into the forward swing. This action creates a delayed hit that sends the ball a long way. Here are four steps to maximizing your power.

Set Up for Power

Set up to the ball in balance, as if you're talking to someone. Flex your knees slightly so you can move.

Your arms should simply hang. Too many amateurs reach with a driver, probably because they think it gives them more power. With a driver, your stance should be wide to maintain power. Use a grip with a hand position that's natural for you. Place your left hand on the club as it hangs and then simply fit the right hand comfortably with the left.

Turn to the Top

To get to the top of the backswing, simply turn your shoulders fully around your spine as you coil the upper body against the lower body. Your weight should not go to the outside of your right foot at the top, nor should the top of your spine tilt toward the target. Make sure you coil your shoulders completely and cock your wrists fully at the top to maximize your distance.

Turn Through to the Finish

From the top, simply turn your body to the finish position. Let everything else follow, maintaining those coiled and cocked power positions as long as you can before impact. Just make an athletic rotation of the body with the arms and hands following as you swing into a balanced finish position. Balance is critical. You can swing as hard as you want, but if you lose balance you'll never hit the ball solidly—or far.

continued

Maintain Spine Angle

Turning around a constant spine angle is the key to good ball striking. You should consider two spine angles—the amount your spine tilts forward from your hips and the amount the spine tilts back, away from the target and ball. The forward spine tilt will not vary from club to club, but you'll tilt farther away from the target and ball with longer clubs.

A good spine angle will help you connect with the ball effectively.

Following Through

You've all seen Gary Player's and Chi Chi Rodriguez's famous walk-through moves as they make contact with the ball. You've watched Arnold Palmer's trademark lean to the left as he wills the ball into the fairway and Jack Nicklaus's traditional, balanced stare as he watches the ball land softly on the green. It's hard to question any of their methods, but at impact, one thing is clear—the follow-through can be an individualized motion. Larry Nelson, who possesses a natural, flowing swing, says this of the follow-through: "I have never really worried about being perfectly balanced at the end of a swing—it's of little importance because the ball is already gone. If your shots are going where you want them to go, you have the proper balance at impact."

Of course, it's easy for a guy who's balanced 98 percent of the time to not worry about the offending 2 percent, but it's a valid point, providing that you have indeed made square contact.

If you haven't grooved your swing and aren't making solid contact, then an aggressive follow-through is even more important. A couple of other factors are involved, too. What once may have been abs of steel are now more like abs of steel wool, and it's getting a little harder to whip those hips around. If you can tighten up the abs and keep the hips looser, it'll help you generate an aggressive turn through the ball that will allow you to rotate the head, chest, and arms through the ball to a high finish. Make the effort to rotate those hips, getting the belt buckle to point to the target, and you'll finish the shot squarely with solid results.

We know that most golfers can't get into the positions that John Daly, Tiger Woods, and so many of their tour peers achieve so effortlessly without having a chiropractor in their foursome. The difference here is that some of those flatbelly wannabes at home are still going to try the maneuvers that the big hitters on the tour employ. Let those young people at the club flail away. If they don't wind up popping a disc, they'll be punching their balls out of the woods as you play your approach shot from the middle of the fairway and put them on the defensive.

Moral of the story? Establish just how much distance you need off the tee to allow you to play your best golf. You

a

Jack Nicklaus *(a)* and Larry Nelson *(b)* are well-balanced in their follow-throughs.

b

obviously want to be in the same zip code as the real long-ball hitters, but not if it comes at the expense of the rest of your game. Length may be important, but only if you can use it to score better.

Although these swing tips might be giving you some big ideas, stay focused on the ultimate goal—fewer bogeys and more pars and birdies. Remember also the other pieces to the puzzle—managing the course and finding the right equipment, for example. We'll cover those topics in later chapters. In the next chapter, however, we shift our focus from generating distance to mastering the short game.

chapter

3

Zeroing In on
the Short Game

Fighting the battle over lost yards? An impeccable short game is the best revenge.

In our thirst for the longest and strongest that manufacturers can assemble, we overlook one thing. Ask players on golf's professional tours—PGA, Senior PGA, or LPGA—and they'll tell you one thing: it's not how far you hit it, it's how many (or more to the point, how few) strokes it takes to get it in the hole. Man or woman, young or old, long or short off the tee, these professionals will say that real success on the golf course comes from 100 yards and in.

So, although we've espoused in the preceding chapters that you should do everything in your power to retain and increase distance and accuracy from the tee and the fairway, we'd also like to remind you that golf is a multifaceted game. We certainly don't want to diminish the importance of practicing full shots. But banging ball after ball on the practice range is like taking an assault rifle to a target range—you might feel better blasting away, but you're going to have a tough time taking that shredded bull's-eye to the judges.

As long as they're keeping score, we might as well try to get the best out of our games. And although everything we've discussed in this book is aimed at keeping your game in tip-top shape, scoring is the name of the game.

How many times have you said, "Well, I didn't hit it very well, but I scored OK." Or, unfortunately, vice versa. As we delve into the subtleties of beating bogey and its ugly cousins, realize that the two items most necessary to short-game development are creativity and practice. You need creativity to pull off the variety of shots that will get you out of the jams you put yourself into with errant approach shots. But creativity without skill will create an even bigger problem—having to make another deft shot to salvage a bogey instead of having a shot at making par. So, coming to grips with a loss of distance over time should lead to its natural conclusion—the short game is king.

With that in mind, let's look at saving strokes, whether from 100 yards or just off the green. The examination will require analysis of every facet of your game, from strategy, shot selection, and execution to how many wedges you need to carry (and whether you should be carrying that lob wedge, which we'll get to later).

We'll provide instruction here, but we must first talk at least briefly about the philosophy of the short game. As we discuss the shots that you must develop and then refine, you must also think about your game and the places where you play your golf. Do you play on a course that is lush and heavily watered, featuring elevated green complexes guarded by bunkers and water? Are the fairways mowed tight and watered sparingly? Do they feature "runways" into every green? Are the greens themselves small and slow, or are they huge, contoured, and more slippery than an uncooperative dog getting a bath?

Most important, you must ask yourself about your expectations. Are you a one-course golfer or do you travel the globe in search of great golf experiences? It's a vital question as you work on this newly important part of your game. If you're going to play only the occasional round away from your home course, then it makes sense to concentrate on refining the skills that will help you succeed at home. But if you're the kind who plays in member-guests all over the place, travels extensively on business, or makes regular trips to check out the new and notable designs, you'll need to have many tools to handle the myriad situations you'll encounter in your rounds away from home.

Who Wants a Better Score?

When you start missing greens, it's important to keep track of how and where you're missing them. A loss of accuracy is something to reclaim on the practice range after you've had a teaching professional check your swing to make sure that your mechanics aren't faulty. But when you start missing greens because you've lost distance, it's time to make other changes. Improving your short game and then developing a strategy to make best use of it will yield lower scores and a boost in confidence each time you tee it up.

When long par-fours become unreachable, it's time to make certain that most times you will still have a chance for a makable par putt. This strategy doesn't mean you're giving up; it means you're charting a course for not giving back any more strokes to par than you have to. If you're in the middle of the fairway with absolutely no hope for getting home, yet still feel it's your duty to take a mighty whack, regardless of the consequences, it's likely that you'll be playing your third shot from a less-than-ideal location. So if you're tired of cold-topping or chunking that approach shot because you put a death grip on your 3-wood (or even worse, tried to hit the driver off the deck), which you swung with the force generally reserved for cutting tall timber, and you groused for the 20-yard walk to the ball and promised never to do it again, then take our advice—*don't do it again.*

There's no ignominy in playing it smart. When you're checking out your options from the fairway—or especially the rough—take a look at what a misplayed shot could do to your score on the hole. Ordinarily, we're not advocates of planting negative seeds in your head, but watching out for trouble is actually a positive way of protecting yourself from blowing up on one or a number of holes, occurrences that could ultimately cost you a good round or even a match. So, from your view to the green, identify the places near the green from which you have the best chance of making par (or even having a good chance at chipping in for birdie). Here's a checklist for making smart decisions:

- Where is the pin?
- Is the slope of the green obvious?

A golf professional can help you develop your swing.

- Where are the hazards?
- What is my normal full-swing shot pattern (and how do I play the shot to prevent the ball from landing in a spot that will make my chip impossible to get close)?
- How close to the green can I get my approach shot without causing a bad swing?

Identifying your tendencies and the need to set yourself up to succeed on a given hole is called course management. Although it might seem a little condescending to identify a term that you've known since Moses was a kid, this not-so-subtle jab is intended not to patronize but to reacquaint you with the concept. Most of us think course management is for wimps, yet we automatically reach for the 3-wood on a god-awful long par-five (despite the sprinklerhead marker that warns, "Don't even think about it") and then get to work on our drop techniques after dumping one into the creek. If this has happened to you more than five times in the last couple of months, then repeat after me, "Course management is for smart golfers, golfers who don't watch their handicaps spike higher than a type-A person's blood pressure during a 5-hour round." The short answer here is obvious—smarter decisions make for lower scores and less frustrated golfers.

As we get into the various shots you're going to have to brush up on to keep scoring better than your years, keep in mind a couple of simple fundamentals:

- Keep your lower body quiet. Shots around the green require small movements, and leg action will only create one more moving part that will throw off the timing necessary for effective chipping.
- Keep your weight evenly distributed or slightly favoring the forward foot.
- Keep your head even or slightly ahead of the ball, a position that allows you to hit against a firm left side (minimizing the wristy swing that results in either chili-dipped or thin-chip chip shots).
- Move your arms as one unit, again minimizing the moving parts of the motion, this time to the keep the upper body solid and free of tension.

a a quiet, still lower body

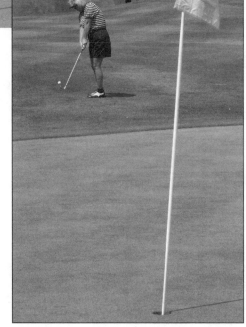

b a smooth, solid motion

Simple fundamentals.

The Pitch

Play this shot with a 9-iron, pitching wedge, or sand wedge, depending on the amount of fairway or green between you and the flagstick. Obviously, the amount of loft among those three clubs will produce either a lower trajectory and more roll or a more lofted approach and enough spin to get the ball to stop more quickly near the flagstick.

The pitch shot.

As previously stated, solid strategy from the fairway will get you in position to have good pitching and chipping opportunities, so take advantage of them. Keeping your lower body and hands quiet is the first step to succeeding. But remember that keeping your hands quiet doesn't mean that you're making a passive effort at the ball. At address, start with your hands a few inches ahead of the ball. This position will minimize the impulse to get wristy. Because the shot requires a crisp swing and a descending blow (it may help you to position the ball in the middle or even a little back in your stance), on the way back hinge your wrists commensurately with the length of the shot. How much is enough? There's only one way to find out, and that's by spending a lot of time at the practice green where you can hone your feel. As you work on your wrist cock, also gauge the feel at impact—keep your wrists solid and square through the ball. As the backswing and follow-through get higher, so too will the trajectory of the ball. Keep your wrists firm and let the ball run to the hole.

You probably remember that old saw, "Let the club do the work." Well, it may be a cliché, but it's indisputable. Trying to scoop the ball is short-game death, so just work on your motion until it feels completely natural. The club is designed to get the ball in the air, so let it.

The Bump-and-Run

You've seen it during every British Open telecast, but it's not exactly a staple at many American golf courses. To play the bump-and-run, you'll need plenty of tight grass between you and the pin. You can play it with whatever low-lofted club you feel comfortable with—generally from a 5- to 8-iron. The technique is virtually identical to the pitch shot, but it does require a lot of eyeballing. You'll need to identify the undulations in the terrain—in the fairway and the green—because this ball is not going to spend much time in the air. It will hold its line like a putt, so be prepared for it to bend a couple of different ways because the fairway may tilt one way to a green that goes another. The one difference in technique is that you'll have virtually no wrist hinge, which is another advantage if the match is on the line and your nerves are a little jangled.

a

The bump-and-run.

b

The Texas Wedge

We'll get to putting in the next chapter, but using the putter from around the green (which in some parts of Scotland and Ireland could include 30 or 40 yards away) is an acquired taste. Like the lob wedge, it's not for everyone. If you are a fair-to-good putter, chances are you're either experienced with this shot or at least comfortable with it when the need arises.

a   using a putter

The Texas wedge.

b   using a 5 wood

Like most delicate shots around the green, this shot requires commitment if you hope to be successful with it. Committing to the shot will let you focus on the task at hand instead of the mechanics of the task. If you assess the pros and cons and decide that putting off the green offers the best chance to get the ball in or near the hole, then you've taken the first step to executing the shot successfully.

As you examine the situation, check out a few important factors:

- How much fringe are you going to have to negotiate before the ball rolls on the green?
- How long is the fringe you have to get through?
- Is the grain of the grass growing away from the green or toward the green?

Checking these three criteria is important in helping you decide whether you can putt the ball through the fringe. If yards of fringe lie between you and the hole or the fringe is higher than an inch or two, you should probably use a lofted short iron, such as an 8- or 9-iron, to get a little more oomph on the ball and enough loft to prevent the ball from getting bogged down in the longer fringe. If the grain of the grass is growing away from the green, you'll need to figure out whether it's too long to negotiate with a putter or would simply require more force than you're comfortable generating with a putter.

Once you've examined your options and decided on the putt, take a few practice strokes to get a feel for the distance, especially if you haven't played the shot recently. The advantage of this shot is that keeping the ball on the ground decreases the margin for error that other risky approach shots could create. Positive thinking is paramount in the short game, and if you're reliving a couple of fat or bladed chips earlier in the round, you're a dead duck! Get a feel for line and distance, then put a good stroke on it and get ready to mark a lower score on the hole. It's vital that you accelerate through the ball to keep it rolling truer once it gets to the green. Getting through the longer fringe will naturally start the ball bouncing more than it would on a smoother green, so concentrate on keeping a crisp tempo back and through the ball.

You may be tempted to try two plays around the green:

- One of the riskier moves with the putter from off the green is using it from out of the bunker. Again, it's possible to make this gamble work, especially if you're in a bunker with no lip and the pin is tucked tightly next to the bunker, a position that would make it tough for even the best bunker player to get it within gimme range. That said, don't get cute just because you think you can pull it off. It's a risk, but if it's a risk you are comfortable attempting, then at least find a practice bunker that fits the bill and work on the shot before taking it to the course.

• And for all of you who saw Chi Chi start the "chipping with the fairway wood" craze, just remember that most of the players you see attempting that shot with any success do it for a living. They have the time and motivation to figure out new ways to get the most shots from every club in the bag. But when amateurs see that on TV on Sunday and then try it on Monday with their pals before they know if they're capable of playing the shot, it's the worst scenario possible. Unless you're willing to put in the time and effort to hone this new shot, you're just showing off. If you're willing to score a bunch of double bogeys to look cool, be our guest. But find out whether that Texas wedge is a viable weapon in your arsenal before you try anything else.

The Lob Shot

The well-executed lob shot is a beautiful sight. The graceful swing, the lilting parabolic trajectory, the remarkable amount of spin, the tap-in putts . . . and for most of us it's all an illusion because we are incapable of hitting the shot! Although we'll never dispute its usefulness in the face of a yawning bunker, bubbling brook, or gnarly cabbage between you and a tightly tucked pin, we'll argue vociferously that— next to the misguided urge to hit the ball farther than any human ever has before—it may be the most dangerous urge in the game.

Still, the technique is important to learn—almost as important as practicing it once you get the secret code—as long as you understand the inherent dangers. We'll discuss merits of the club in greater detail below, but because the 60-degree wedge is the stick most golfers are placing in their bags as a third wedge, we'd like to suggest that you compromise on the most lofted wedge in your set. To add another club that you might use more, you should consider using a 57- or 58-degree wedge as your sand wedge. It will cost you a little distance from your regular 55- or 56-degree sand wedge, but it will provide enough loft to let you open up the face and use it like the lob wedge.

The lob shot.

Now that the anti-60 portion of the program has ended (for now), let's talk about actually hitting the shot. Again, you should distribute your weight evenly at address and not really change the distribution significantly through the swing. The swing itself is virtually identical to a bunker shot. The length and tempo of the swing will vary with the distance you need to cover. As with the pitch shots, the length of the wrist cock at the top of the swing and the height of your

Follow-through determines trajectory: low hands, low trajectory.

hands on the follow-through will dictate the height of the shot.

Now that we have the motion down, let's discuss impact. In the deeper rough, you'll want to swing through the grass behind the ball, essentially "splashing" through the grass as you would through sand. If you keep your left arm firm through impact, you'll maintain acceleration through the ball and guarantee that it will fly higher and land softer.

Follow-through determines trajectory: high hands, high trajectory.

The Lob Wedge

Seve Ballesteros says we don't need one, that a 56-degree sand wedge provides enough flexibility to open the face and lob a shot, close the face and knock a shot into the green and make it spin, or play it straight and take a controlled, full

Tommy Jacobs using the lob wedge from a clean lie.

swing, letting the loft do its job, in the sand or out. Of course, this sounds so logical coming from a man with hands like Picasso's, a man for whom no attempt is too risky, a man who refined his skills by simply having been under innumerable tree branches or opposite fairways in the past 30 years.

Tommy Jacobs using the lob wedge from deeper rough.

It is also said in every self-defense class that you should never carry a weapon that you're unprepared to have used on you—in other words, if you're going to pull a gun on someone, you'd better hope they don't wrestle it out of your hands. It may be a bleak example, but hey, a little short-game hyperbole can go a long way.

In our humble opinion, the lob wedge may well be the single-best stroke-saving tool ever invented. We also believe, however, that about 90 percent of golfers should never consider putting them in their bags. We'd even go so far as to lobby Congress on behalf of deluded golfers everywhere. That may be a little harsh, but if we can't be brutally honest with each other at this point, then you're never going to come to grips with aging and you probably stopped paying attention to our cajoling and nudging several chapters ago.

Several things can happen with a lob wedge:

• You do your best Phil Mickelson imitation, take a full swing from 20 yards away, and watch the ball become a balata parachute, opening high and landing softer than a baby's bottom as it nestles next to the pin (likelihood: 1 in 10,000).

• You try for the Phil Mickelson but wind up with the Phil Lebowski, a chili dip of Biblical proportions. Of course, you could look on the bright side—you'll get a chance to try it again, immediately, because you're still away, and now you're in that bunker you were trying to avoid in the first place.

• You lose your nerve halfway into the backswing, the downswing gets out of whack, and you blade the ball into the creek that runs behind the green, or even worse, send the foursome on the next tee scattering.

• You create the spin you so admire in those tour players, but the green is sloping toward you and the ball winds up back at your feet, which means you were hitting the club because you're good at it, not because it was the right shot to play.

Three out of four doesn't look so good, does it?

This is a wonderful, magical, revolutionary piece of equipment at our fingertips. If you are set on carrying it in your bag, practice with it diligently and find out what your strengths and limitations with it are. Know exactly how far you hit it, how much spin you can generate, and how comfortable you feel with it when the round or match is on the line. But don't say we didn't warn you!

Now that you have made it from the fairway to the green, let's examine putting. After all, what good does it do if you can put it on the green but can't finish in the hole?

4

Conquering
the Greens

As you've continued to read through this book, you're likely finding yourself in one of three scenarios.

1. Best-case scenario—the exhilarating realization that you have the time, inclination, and tools to play a lot of golf.
2. Middling scenario—the understanding that although you're making a couple of loose swings each round and you're not as infallible as you once were, you can get your game in shape.
3. Worst-case scenario—your game has gone south faster than a Lotto winner with a new girlfriend, and you haven't the vaguest idea how to get it back over the border.

These realizations, rationalizations, and exhortations may be coming from your desire to reclaim your game (the aforementioned best-case scenario) or through some previously unforeseen forces that have conspired to take away your long game—your iron play—and have left you stranded without a short game (the all-too-familiar worst-case scenario). Ah, but here's the opening—all golfers 50 and over can get their revenge by becoming as close to automatic as possible on the greens.

The Importance of Putting

Whether we admit it or not, most of us have long overlooked just how important putting is in our games. It's faulty logic at its worst—we don't putt well and just chalk it up to not being a natural with the flat stick. So most of the players who don't immediately find success on the greens "work" on their putting only after they've stretched, hit balls, chipped, and fumbled through their bags for their lucky ballmarker and a few tees. They half-heartedly slap the ball at the hole with one eye on the groups on the tee and the other on the beverage cart. Then after missing a couple of four-footers in the first few holes, they consider themselves doomed for the rest of the round.

But for those who've been around the game for most of your lives, do you remember a time when you felt that you were simply incapable of missing a single putt? Be honest with yourself and you'll realize that you were a great putter when you were a kid. Why? Because while you were waiting either for a loop in the caddie yard or for your parents or friends to go out to tee it up, you were putting on the practice green for pennies, nickels, or dimes with your other pals. Those brief contests made you a better putter for a couple of reasons—you were motivated to get some spending money in your pocket, and you wanted bragging rights among your peers. You putted with a purpose, with concentration and goal-oriented determination. Of course, it may have helped that the concept of stress hadn't yet prowled into your subconscious.

Ask yourself how it was different today—as you lament your lost sense of speed and direction—and you'll get the harsh answer that's been true for the better part of your adult life in golf. You get to the club 90 minutes before your tee time to get loose. You hit a garbage pail full of balls and don't leave the tee until you hear, ". . . and next on the tee . . ." Then you knock three or four balls in the general vicinity of the hole while chatting up your partners about their dinners the night before and your grandkid's school play. Look, the saying hasn't changed in the decades that you've paid attention to this aspect of your game: nearly half of the shots that make up your final score come on the putting green.

Now, what are you going to do about it?

Putting is a vital part of your game even if your style is a bit unorthodox.

Contact Sport

As we discuss what could be wrong with your putting stroke—
and indeed there could be myriad things—the simplest of them
all is that you're not making square contact. This is simple, to
be sure, and it's no different from any of our discussions about
getting the best results from your full swing. But the concept
may be even more important in putting than in playing those
full shots.

Think about it. In most cases, you can get away with loose
swings here and there on full shots because you have plenty
of terrain to aim for and from which to hit recovery shots. On
the greens, however, you're obviously dealing with a shorter
piece of property. Add to this the fact that you must cover the
route to the hole solely along the ground, and every facet of the
process is magnified. You have to read the terrain, gauge the
speed of the greens, and play the shot. And we haven't even
gotten into the mental stuff—your standing in the match or
tournament, your opportunity to shoot the best round of the
(pick one) week, month, or year, your previous three-putts,
your aggressiveness, and your work or home problems piling
up in your subconscious. And we haven't even discussed
whether you fully trust yourself yet.

Putting is anguish. It's immediate gratification or alienation,
often in the same putt. You strike it well, it's online the entire
way to the hole, and then it either stops a half revolution from
dropping into the hole or curls inside the cup before stopping
precisely in the spot you thought it actually was about to drop
into in the first place. Then the wayward putt gets in your head,
and you're left stewing about it on the way to the next tee or,
even worse, the next time you have to hit a putt.

OK, we have to deal with the psychology of putting. We've
gotten some of the emotional baggage out of the way already,
but it's time to reach the logical conclusion to getting to, or
getting back to, success on the greens—you must put yourself
in the best position to make the putt or at least stroke the ball
well enough to hear two of the best words in any language,
"That's good." Making square contact with the ball is the best
start on the road to putting success. And although few full
swings are identical, putting strokes really run the gamut—

wide or narrow stance; front or back ball position; hands together or hands apart; open, neutral, or closed stance; flowing stroke or erratic jab.

"Whatever works" is a standard response, and it's a good response—when you're putting well. When you're not, however, a putting stroke that defies convention and the simple rules of physics is a heavy burden. Therefore, let's understand a few things.

- "It works for me." If it did, you wouldn't be here looking for answers.
- "My pro doesn't think I should change my stroke." That's because you ignore his or her advice or are in denial.
- "This grip and stance came to me last night when I was in bed." In the words of the immortal Jimmy Breslin, "Never trust an idea unless it survives the hangover."

Golf professionals would not stress the fundamentals every day of their lives if they didn't know it was the right thing to do.

Dave Stockton, one of the best putters in professional golf for generations and winner of 14 senior tour events and close to $8 million solely on the senior circuit, says that observing a few guidelines will automatically improve your putting:

- Move the ball back in your stance. Stockton asserts that getting the ball back toward the middle of your stance—at least three inches from your front heel—will allow you to have better control on your putts. "Changing your ball position will keep the backswing controlled while also allowing you to bring the club forward with the same amount of follow-through and improved pace to promote a smoother roll on the putt."

- Keep the putter low back and through the ball. "If you let the putter get too far off the ground on the backswing—and especially on the way back to the ball—you're probably not going to make square contact, which will make it pretty much impossible to get a true roll on the ball, which means you'll have a tough time getting in anywhere near the hole."

- Keep your hands high. "If you're not getting the ball anywhere near the hole, chances are you're too far away from the ball, which in turn pushes your hands too low, resulting in pulled putts. If you move just a couple of inches closer to the ball, you're hands will get higher, the shaft will get closer to vertical, and your eyes will be directly over the ball. You'll get a better look at the putt and will be more comfortable."

• Die the ball at the hole. Call him the anti-Watson. "Guys like Watson, Palmer, and Tiger like to ram the ball into the back of the cup and while that works for them, I'm afraid it doesn't for most amateur golfers. If you can get your putts to die into the hole, you won't have to worry about the power lipouts when the ball comes right back at you. Concentrate on the read and the speed of the putt, pour it over the front edge of the cup, and you'll have a chance to use the hole cup to your advantage."

Speed and Direction

You may have noticed over the years that you don't judge speed as well as you once did. You have a tougher time getting a solid read on the putt, and you're having difficulty making the short ones. You may have one or more symptoms, all of which may appear periodically or together. It may seem elementary, but it's important to get regular eye exams—for your everyday life, certainly, but especially for your golf game. Once you get those peepers checked out, talk to your doctor about contact lenses or even the laser surgery that has been so popular among players on the senior tour. Hale Irwin and Tom Kite are the latest players to get the laser treatment. Both have said that after a short readjustment period, they've never had more confidence that their eyes wouldn't play tricks on them. If the thought of anyone coming near your eyes with anything stronger than eyedrops makes your skin crawl, check out the latest development in lineless bifocals, which should help keep things in perspective as you look down at a putt.

Once you get the eyes fixed, you're ready to concentrate on how exactly you're going to eliminate those nasty three-putts. Dave Pelz, the man with the encyclopedic collection of putting and short-game data, the man most touring professionals turn to when they're losing sleep and their minds (not necessarily in that order) over their short games, says comfort is the first key to improvement on the greens. "You must be comfortable to be a good putter—practice and good mechanics will follow." Pelz asserts that at least 80 percent of amateurs miss their putts on the low side of the hole, never giving the ball a true shot at going in. He asserts that a big part of the problem stems from players who favor an open stance for putts, which he says is certain to create pulled putts. He notes that some of the problems might also be the result of improperly fitting equipment. "Too many guys try to make their address fit their putter," Pelz says. "This produces address positions that make a good fundamental stroke exceptionally difficult."

Again, as we stress the root of all that is evil in poor putting—glancing contact—you must do everything possible to groove that solid, repeatable motion. Concentrate on a solid, simple pendulum motion, keeping the putter square just before, at, and immediately after impact. Pelz and teaching professionals around the globe also stress the importance of building a habit similar to the ritual that a basketball player grooves for foul shooting or the series of actions that a field-goal kicker executes before making the kick that counts. By making the preparation and stroke second nature, you will take nerves, uncertainty, and unwanted results out of the equation.

Drills and Preparation

If you're serious about saving strokes on the green, you'll have to work on the skills necessary for improving. Your workload isn't limited to the putting green, either. If you've noticed a little less control when the club is in your hands, it's time to get some of that old strength back. Now, we're not saying you need Hal Sutton forearms, but a couple of simple strategies will help get you back in the game. While you're watching television or reading a book, get a tennis ball and squeeze repeatedly. You can do it either by count or by a time limit before switching hands. If you don't have any tennis balls lying around the house, once you've finished reading the paper and doing the crossword puzzle, put a single sheet of newsprint on the table. Then, with just one hand, ball it up until you've made it as small a ball as you possibly can. Doing this will certainly produce some strange piles for the recycling truck, but it'll improve strength in the hands, fingers, and forearms, which will help you keep the putter square as well as improve your contact on full shots.

Several other tips can help you stay on top of your putting:

• Spend an entire practice session with just one ball. Hit it until you get it in the hole. Do it repeatedly and don't cheat yourself—no gimmes and no I-would-have-made-its. This will give you a chance to learn your tendencies as well as work on putts of varying lengths.

This simple exercise will improve the strength of your forearms, hands, and fingers.

• Put a half-dozen balls around the hole in a 20-foot circle and either try to make them or get them within tap-in range. Once you're comfortable with your stroke, move in 5 feet. Repeat the process all the way to a 5-foot circle. From the 5-foot circle, don't leave until you make every putt.

Putting drills are a great way to improve your accuracy and confidence on the greens.

• Practice long putts as well as short putts. Chances are you're going to have a bunch of 20-footers during a round, so become comfortable with your ability to get the ball into "that's good" range.

• Practice getting long putts close to the hole by putting a few tees roughly two feet on either side of, and behind, the hole. Keep hitting putts until you are knocking one after another into that "trough."

Above all, remain positive and committed to improving your putting. It's the quickest way to shave strokes off your score and the best way to improve your chances of taking your friends' money.

The Right Cross?

Many players who've been struggling or just looking for a little edge to get them over the hump consider making the switch to the cross-handed putting stroke. The tours likely have great influence on most of us—we see close-ups of players grinding it out over a putt for $650,000 and the win, and we notice the left hand below the right and think, "Well, if he can stay in the top 10 in season earnings, maybe it'll help me take five bucks off Smitty."

And the short answer is that you may be right. As we've discussed, despite fundamentals that must be adhered to, putting is a subjective endeavor. Experimentation is inherent in the pursuit of saving strokes on the greens, and there's no reason for you not to try it if you think it could give you a boost. As always, we recommend that you head to the practice green and work on the fundamentals of a good cross-handed stroke before you use it in your game.

One of the strengths of the cross-handed grip is that it levels the shoulders. If you have trouble with an open stance or pulling your putts, this grip and a square stance will help you stay square to the hole on straight putts or square to the line on longer breaking putts. The cross-handed grip also promotes a solid left hand, which will keep you from "cupping" or breaking your left wrist at impact and follow-through, actions that will hamper your speed and line. This method can also help you keep the putterface low back and through the ball, promoting a smoother roll on the ball and thus a chance to get the ball started on a better path to the hole.

The cross-handed putting stroke.

If you're going to try the cross-handed stroke, don't look at it as a give-up strategy. This is a solid alternative if you think you need to make a change in your stroke, so don't just think of it as a bandage for your troubles with the short stick. Commit to your goals for improving your putting, work on this technique and the changes you'll need to adjust to in the stroke, and you might be picking more balls out of the cup.

Model Citizens

You've tried everything. Your basement is full of the alleged latest and greatest that puttermakers could produce. But where were those designers and engineers when your friends decided to hold a locker-room intervention in which they told you that the putter with which you'd just three-putted 13 greens had to be dumped in a trash compactor to ensure that you'd never use it again? That said, if the old rusty blade from that set of circa-1954 Sam Snead Blue Ridge clubs does the trick, then don't let anyone tell you different. But one of the developments in short sticks over the last few years is that some of those "short sticks" no longer are.

The advent of the long shaft with the split grip was prompted by two factors—a lack of success with a conventional putter and bad backs that made hunkering down over a four-footer nearly impossible. Although those two things aren't necessarily linked, they are legitimate concerns. The long putter will help players with bad backs maintain a disciplined stroke—provided they work with the longer club to groove a repeatable stroke—while keeping them free of pain and concerns over what could happen if they did twist the wrong way or get hunched over the ball only to have trouble getting back up.

Don't Get Jumpy

If you're feeling anxious on the greens, you're not alone. You have plenty of reasons on a good day to feel tight out there with nothing but short grass between you and the hole, so you should do everything in your power to keep yourself in control before you even hit your first putt. Caffeine can present a real impediment to success on the greens, so take it out of your preround ritual and give yourself a fighting chance to sink a couple of putts. Pass on the coffee and tea in favor of juice or hot water with lemon. Remember that chocolate has plenty of caffeine, too, so put down that doughnut in favor of some fresh fruit or cereal before the round. When you're making the turn, grab a banana instead of that candy bar—you'd hate to throw away those smart decisions you made before the round by ruining the back nine because you had a sugar craving halfway through the round.

Besides avoiding the foods that can cause trouble on the greens, try to eliminate the outside pressures and extraneous thoughts that can sap your concentration. Take a deep breath and shake the tension from your arms as you take a practice swing. Slowly let out the air before you get over the ball to make the putt. Jack Nicklaus, the best clutch putter professional golf has ever produced, says that he frequently holds his breath in order to remain still over the stroke.

If you've done all the things you can to keep yourself on an even keel yet still remain as nervous as a cat in the dog pound, just remember what Lee Trevino said: "Putting for big fat paychecks on tour isn't pressure. Pressure is putting for a $10 match when you only have $5 in your pocket." Simply put, don't get yourself into money matches you have no business competing in. If you don't have the dough to play for, then just make a friendly wager with your playing partners. If money's not the issue and you're just hypercompetitive and can't stand the thought of opening your wallet for the first time since the Carter administration, then lighten up. It's just a game (yeah, right).

Jack Nicklaus sinking another clutch putt.

The Dread Disease

When things go bad on the greens, what emerges is the most pervasive, insidious malady any of us can imagine. Trying to make sense of the yips—whether in these pages or around the table with your golf buddies—is about the most uncomfortable discussion that golfers can have with one another.

When "the troubles" begin, it seems that nothing that can pull you from the abyss of negativity—your stroke disappears, your concentration heads for points unknown, and nobody will shake your hand or pat you on the back for fear of catching what you have. Johnny Miller, one of the best ball strikers in golf, says that he had little interest in playing on the senior tour because, besides his battle with a variety of old injuries, he didn't want to put his miserable putting stroke on display again. "And I've got news for you," he said. "It's a good thing I used to hit the ball so close to the stick years ago, because I wasn't a much better putter back then either."

But make no mistake: although the yips get inside your head and threaten to ruin every repetitive function you perform during a day, it's really about mechanics. That's where it all starts. If you made one flawless stroke after another and the ball just kept burning the edges, you could find a way to live with yourself until the ball started going back into the hole. But when you can't keep the ball anywhere near the clubface and wind up in some sort of spasm, lurching at the ball and hoping to get it halfway to the hole, it's impossible to believe that an end will ever come to the malady.

Quite simply, when you feel the yips coming on, get yourself to a golf professional, get back on track physically, and practice your technique diligently until you can rid yourself of the dark cloud enveloping you.

We in no way intend to minimize the gravity of the situation; indeed, the goal here is to be clinical in your diagnosis of the problem and its cure. If you keep the dissection of the breakdown in your technique simple, it will in some way help to deflect the mental effects of not being able to pull the putter back, not getting the ball anywhere near the line or the hole. The yips is a golfer's disease, not just an older golfer's disease. Concentrate on developing and maintaining proper technique with your putting stroke and try to keep the yips at bay. As Nicklaus says, "Believe you can make 'em and you frequently will."

Now that you have control of the long game, the short game, and your putter, let's examine the way you attack the course as a whole.

A golf pro can help you overcome the yips.

chapter

5

Managing the Course

The way you manage your play on the course truly reflects your attitude toward the game. If you want to be the best player you can be, you must be aware of your capabilities and find effective strategies for navigating your way around the course. This means you have to be realistic about your game and set goals that are within your reach. Course management starts with your ability to control your emotions and think clearly throughout a round. If you're mentally in control on the course, you'll be able to develop a successful strategy for each shot and each hole.

The first goal is to establish a pattern and structure for thinking your way around the course. A good starting point is to consider the course as 18 separate trials rather than a single grand challenge or two 9-hole tests. Within each of these 18 challenges you'll face similar problems, but you'll need an organized, objective way to approach each of them. By using a routine, you can assess the risks you're taking on a hole by hole basis. Every hole is designed to tempt you or tease you in some way, and you must face the challenge in a way that will keep the numbers low on your scorecard. Each shot you make has the possibility of not working out the way you wanted it to. So you must be able to start again, to reassess the situation before making the next shot.

You've probably heard the expression "percentage golf," a decision-making approach in which the player considers the options for each shot and chooses the strategy that presents the best risk based on his or her skill level and consistency. In this chapter, we'll examine the elements of a strong strategy and teach you how to read the course.

Driving Strategy

They say you putt for dough—and you can certainly save many strokes around the greens—but winning golf starts with smart play from the tee. Although the tee-box area is usually just a few yards wide, you can use it to your advantage in many ways, particularly mentally. Ask yourself the following questions.

Where Do You Want to Hit Your Drive?

First, you must establish the ideal place to put your drive. High handicappers are often happy just to keep the ball in play; others may focus on a 40-yard circle. But regardless of your skill level, you should use the target to create your alignment and play the hole positively.

One useful step is to think ahead to your second shot. The best target from the tee is the place from which you'd like to play your next shot. But you also have to assess the danger of not making the perfect shot from the tee. It may seem pessimistic, but being realistic about your skills is one of the keys to maximizing your game.

For every tee shot, you should consider two or three possible shots and their possible outcomes. Option number 1 could put you in the best position, but it probably carries the highest risk. Option number 2 may not set you up as well for your second shot but could considerably reduce the risk of a mishit from the tee. Option number 3 may be the most conservative, offering the longest route to the hole, but if you're not playing well it may be the best way to rebuild your confidence and have an opportunity to score well.

Play smart from the tee!

What Are the Angles?

Golf is a game of angles—everything from your grip and alignment to the angle and direction of the hole. If you have a mathematical mind, you'll probably stand on the tee and consider the angles of the hole and the shortest path to the green.

The shortest route, however, may also be the most dangerous play. It's always worthwhile to sacrifice a few yards to hit to a safer landing area.

What Are the Conditions?

Many players overlook the wind, water, sand, rough, and trees. Although these elements are sometimes difficult to see, the smart player gauges wind direction and speed from flags fluttering and trees moving, notes the composition of the grass, considers the thickness of the rough—all the factors that contribute to ball flight and shotmaking ability.

Wisely assessing course conditions before you address the ball will keep you out of the rough.

DRIVING STRATEGY TIPS

Graham Marsh

Good scoring starts before you tee up on every hole. Many golfers think that driving simply means hitting the ball as far as they can. They see the driver as a "distance object." I don't think of it that way at all. To me, driving is a means of putting the ball into play in the best possible position from which to hit the next shot. I view the driver as a utility club.

I always tell my amateur playing partners not to trust the tee—or the tee markers. You will not believe how often I see players make the fundamental mistake of automatically lining up square to the direction the tee is pointing or to the tee markers themselves. This misstep costs them many strokes without their realizing it. Make certain to select your best landing area and line up to it precisely, no matter where the tee is pointing. Ignore the alignment of the tee box and tee markers.

Tee-box strategy is fundamental.

Your Approach

Once you're at the stage to hit an approach to the green, you have additional factors to consider. You must deal with the delicate speed of the green and its contours and traps. The typical course-management question in this situation is, "Should I attempt to attack the flag or play to a safe part of the green?"

To help you decide which club to pull, you'll have to assess the following.

- Wind. What is the average wind direction and speed? Is it gusting? You will see professionals spending a great deal of time trying to gauge wind speed and direction. Watch the flag and the tops of trees to determine how much wind is blowing in the fairway ahead of you. Into the wind, you may need to attempt to hit the ball low.

- Lie. If you're hitting from rough or no grass, it's unlikely that you will be able to get the clubface to grip the ball and give you power or control of the shot.

- Distance. You can determine your distance to either the front or middle of the green by using yardage markers. From there, you can weigh the other conditions of the shot and decide how they will affect your club choice.

- Pin placement and shape of the green. The placement of the pin will affect both your distance and the type of shot you want to play. If the flag is at the back of the green, you may be able to land the ball on the front and let it roll to the back depending on the softness or slope of the green. The question is, where do you want to land the ball? Depending on how high you hit the ball, you may need to consider how quickly you need to stop the ball on the green. If the flag is only five yards from the front of the green with a water hazard just in front of the green, you'll need a lofted club to stop the ball near the hole. Conversely, you may have 40 yards of green in front of the flag. In that case, you may have more luck rolling the ball toward the hole with a less-lofted club. Only advanced players can shape shots to get the ball closer to the target, but everyone should consider pin placement and its relationship to the shape, angle, and direction of the green.

• Contours of the green. Sometimes it's better to be 20 feet below the hole than 3 feet above it because of the contours and shape of the green. An uphill putt is easier to judge for speed and direction, so you should usually plan your shot to stop the ball below the hole. If the green is sloped, you also have to judge how the contour will affect your shot.

• The hazards surrounding the green. If you miss the green, where do you want to miss? It may seem like a negative question, but it's worth considering if your short game has obvious weaknesses. If bunkers were located on the left of the green and thick rough on the right, where would you rather be? Top players often prefer the sand. Your lie in the rough could be terrible; the sand usually offers a more consistent lie.

• The risk-reward factor. What overall chance do you have of making the shot based on your past performance. Is it worth the risk? Far too many players play a shot that they'll realistically make once in 10 attempts. When we watch the strategies of professional players, we can lose sense of the best options for ourselves.

STRATEGY

Hale Irwin

You have a short-iron shot to a hole tucked behind a bunker and not much green to work with. It's tempting to shoot for the flag, but if you fall short you'll face a difficult bunker shot, and if you go long you'll have to pitch back out of the rough. In almost every case it's best to play out to the right to the fat part of the green. You'll always have the chance to hole that long putt.

No player on the senior tour has proved to be more of a strategist than Hale Irwin. Let's take a lesson from him on one his strategic strengths—long-iron play.

LONG-IRON PLAY

Hale Irwin

With the popularity of fairway metalwoods, players are hitting fewer long irons than ever. And although there's good sense in hitting a club with which you're comfortable, learning how to hit the long irons can add another dimension to your game. Irons create more backspin than woods, giving you better distance control and workability. More important, for those of you who play in breezy conditions, the long irons are great for keeping the ball low and out of the wind.

In large part, hitting long irons is about attitude. Many people are so afraid of the longer sticks that they instantly opt for a shorter club or a fairway wood. I think that's one reason so many amateurs find themselves splashing down into green-front bunkers and water hazards. They're so convinced that the 7-iron is easier to hit than the 6 or that the 5-wood has to be easier to hit than the 2-iron that they usually end up where most of the trouble is—short right or short left. I'm certain that with a little practice the following tips can help you learn to love your long irons, too.

Here are some steps to simplifying your long-iron shots.

Clear Your Head

People who are intimidated by their long irons often ask me how to hit them. Start with your mind. When you lose your confidence standing over a long iron, that's strictly a mental proposition. I've always thought of my 1-, 2-, 3- and 4-irons as extensions of the pitching wedge. We often hear television commentators refer to the 8-, 9-, and pitching wedge as scoring clubs, but it's important to think of your long irons as scoring clubs too.

Keep It Simple

The swing plane of a long iron may be a tad flatter than that of a short club, but I try not to become hung up on mechanics, particularly in my backswing. I prefer to think about results, about my target. If you ask most amateurs what they think about over the ball, they'll mention grip, stance, and wrist cock, where they're going to take it, the plane of the swing, that they have to be connected. I'll bet only one in a hundred will say, "Well, I want to hit the ball in this part of the fairway," or "I want to put the ball in the hole." Think results.

Now, obviously the backswing is important, but how many odd-looking backswings have we seen at the top levels of the game? How about Jim Furyk, Miller Barber, or Doug Sanders in his day. Look at Jack Nicklaus's flying right elbow. All these players have odd or unique backswings, but they all look tidy at impact.

A long iron requires a slightly wider stance. Ball position may vary as the clubs get longer. You can see that I play a long-iron shot just inside my forward heel. But my long-iron setup and swing are nearly identical to those I use with my shorter clubs. Other than a slight difference in ball position and stance width, the moves are the same.

continued

Checkpoint

At address I try to get my left shoulder higher than the right, but comfortably so. I want to start in the hitting position and on the downswing return to that position at impact.

Up or Down

Contrary to what you may hear, you should hit every long-iron shot with a descending blow. When you try to hit the ball on an ascending path, you're more likely to lift your upper body. The descending blow encourages a full turn and a complete weight shift. How can you make sure you're making contact with a downward blow? Put a tee in the line between your forward heel and the ball. Play a shot. If your divot is entirely in front of the tee, you're making a good downward blow. If your divot is mostly behind the tee, you're making ball contact too late. Remember that golf is a game of opposites. In this case, hit down on the ball and it goes up. Hit up and it will inevitably stay down.

Shift Weight Forward

I see many amateurs who, with a long iron in their hands, feel the urge to lift the ball. They see that flatter clubface and do what I call "fire and fall back," hitting almost entirely off the back foot. This can result in serious mis-hits, not to mention a sore back. Here's a little-known fact: the average 2-iron has more loft than the average 4-wood. For instance, my 2-iron has a 20-degree loft. The loft on my 4-wood is only 17 or 18 degrees. The fact is that a good, active swing will get the ball up. The loft is low for a reason—to make the ball fly low and far. Trying to lift the ball in the air by falling backward prevents the club from doing what it's designed to do. It's a cliché, but it's important—let the club do the work. Place the same trust in the 3-iron that you do in a wedge and you'll notice immediate results.

Swing Through It

Instinct tells us to chop down for power, but for too many people the long-iron swing is a hacking move from shoulder to ground, an action that usually produces disaster. If you try to see the golf swing as more a back-to-front movement than an up-to-down movement, always thinking target and results, you'll see a difference.

Walk On By

Many amateurs have a hard time staying down and through on a long iron. I recommend this drill. It's something I was doing long before my friend Gary Player made it famous—the hit-and-step-through routine. Simply step down the line of flight with your rear foot immediately after impact. I sometimes have people try it at clinics to help them get that backside to come around. This sensation, the idea of having your belt buckle facing the target, is what turning through the ball is all about.

Choke Up

If you want to overcome long-iron phobia, try choking up a little. In the photo shown here, I've choked up on a 4-iron to make it about the length of a 7-iron. Hitting some practice shots while gradually sliding your hands back up the grip can reinforce the notion that a long iron doesn't have to be intimidating.

continued

Let the Shaft Flex Its Muscle

When amateurs have a distant target they automatically give in to the feeling that they have to hit the ball harder. You don't have to swing those long irons any harder than you do a short iron. Don't forget that shafts have flex in them. Even longer shafts, if swung correctly, will get the job done.

When Wood You?

Despite my success with long irons, I occasionally opt for a wood. Today's metalwoods have so much weight in the bottom of the club that they cut through rough better than the woods of old. In the rough, I might take out my 4-wood because it can slip through the grass a little better and I can probably get better contact than I can from a long iron. But if the lie is good, and I have to choose between a 4-wood and a 2-iron, I'm going to hit the iron every time.

Think Like an Architect

One way to improve your knowledge of the game and help you devise strategies is to think like the course architect. Why were the bunkers placed where they are? Why is the fairway sloped the way it is? Why was that tree left there? Once you appreciate how the architect is trying to make you think, you'll consider golf a game of chess, with you dueling the course architect. Challenge yourself to outwit the architect, to avoid the temptations of the course.

Adrenaline

Keep a check on your adrenaline. If you're playing well, your heart rate slowly increases, and your ego can lead you to believe that you're capable of any shot. It's likely that you'll try shots beyond your reach. When you're playing well, a good swing comes without much thought, and you can easily slip into a false sense of security. A cool head can save you from disaster, so be aware that your heart rate affects your thinking on the course.

Full Shots and Half Shots

Skilled players often experiment by using a variety of clubs in similar situations, and so can you. If you hit your wedge about 100 yards, try hitting several clubs the same distance. Grip a 7- or 5-iron slightly farther down the shaft and try to hit a ball the same distance. How well can you judge distances using half or three-quarter shots? In windy conditions you'll find it useful to hit the ball low by punching it into the wind. Using less than a full swing will improve your feel for your clubs, and you will put less stress on your body by not always making full swings.

Whether you're on the senior tour or a 36-handicapper, you use the same principles when it comes to strategy. Be realistic and play to your strengths. Hale Irwin has been a master of long irons for years, so despite the recent trend toward metalwoods for longer approach shots, he still knows how to use long irons to his advantage.

Think of every shot as an opportunity to play smart. Take the time to plan your approach to the hole.

As we head into the next chapter to talk about your equipment, don't get crazy and think that we're going to recommend those 54-inch shafts that Rocky Thompson uses on the senior tour. The only thing you'll need those for is fly-fishing. Turn the page and we'll figure out how to get you in the right gear.

6

Choosing the Right Equipment

You'll do almost anything to play better golf. You'll eat better, you'll exercise, you'll even take a lesson and then practice the things you learned. But there's always that little devil on your shoulder saying, "Pssst, over here, look at me. I'm shiny, built by brilliant guys (many of whom left the foundering aeronautical industry to work in golf, so they know something about getting much bigger things in the air than a golf ball), and I promise that you'll hit the golf ball farther and straighter, and by extension, will be a better person. Expensive? C'mon, how can you put a price tag on low round of the year?"

Don't fault yourself for being tempted. It's a natural reaction, and it's not an altogether new phenomenon either, is it? Face it, you bit on the first Bullseye you saw, got apoplectic over the PowerBilt persimmon, jumped on the Ram Accubars, cared meticulously for those Wilson Staff blades (which you swore you'd never, ever give up), and hired an attack dog to guard your Ping Eye2 irons in the garage. Today you still have that attack dog, sleeping at the foot of your bed, primarily because you've got so much golf equipment crammed into your garage that you haven't been able to squeeze a car in there since the Nixon administration.

It's easy to become passionate about golf clubs. After all, anything that can help us perform up to, and beyond, our capabilities is easily worth the price tag. But as you already know, that price tag is getting heavier and harder to justify, no matter how consumed you are by improving your scores. After a bad round, you find yourself rooting around in the garage looking for the magic wand, the set of irons you sent into exile for a reason you can't remember, the dozens of drivers and wedges that you couldn't squeeze an extra yard out of or couldn't get to stop at the hole. And let's not even consider some of the sins of the putters.

When choosing a club, you have many options. Be prepared to use a variety of clubs in a variety of situations.

While you stroll down memory lane, you look at those clubs as if you were looking at yearbook pictures of old sweethearts, wondering what they could have done so wrong to have not made it with you for the long haul. And while that may be true, you also wore Chuck Taylor's to play basketball, wore a baseball mitt that today would serve as a dress glove, and wore a facemask that gave any opponent with bad intentions a clear shot at making your nose look like a gob of Silly Putty. So, like every other sport, golf has constantly evolved as science has advanced.

You Can't Buy a Game . . . Or Can You?

To borrow from the real estate racket, three words express our innermost gratitude for better golf: technology, technology, technology.

In the past 10 years, the golf equipment category has grown from a solid business to a $2 billion dollar industry. Much of the credit is due to Gary Adams, the late inventor of the Taylor Made metalwood, who pioneered the concept and bankrolled his venture with a high-stakes golf match and a car trunk full of prototypes. Ely Callaway refined the concept and created a marketing-driven juggernaut that's captured the attention of the world and pushed established, traditional equipment manufacturers into the 21st century. But even as clubheads get larger and more expensive, as research and development departments mix metals and metal matrixes to build lighter, stronger, and more performance-driven clubs, and as consumers get savvy enough to discuss these properties with a semblance of understanding—still, it all comes down to you. These new products are good, many of them are even great, but none of them will work unless you're committed to making them work.

Frank Thomas, the head of research and product testing for the United States Golf Association, says that, "every club a golfer buys has a 45-day grace period. What I mean by that is that every golfer is completely committed to that club they've spent their hard-earned money on. They like the way it looks, the way it sounds, and they're committed to doing everything

Maximize your strengths with clubs that fit.

in their power to make the club yield results and, by extension, justify that purchase. Then the day comes when the time is up and the club turns back into a pumpkin."

Still, Thomas's comments shouldn't make the search for the right equipment seem futile. If you are committed to playing your best, you should try as many types of clubs as you see *fit*. And yes, we emphasize that word *fit* for a reason. You will be surprised at two things—how many golfers have ill-fitting clubs and how capable we all are of adapting a less-than-perfect swing to accommodate those less-than-perfect tools. The club-fitting process today is a sophisticated procedure that will allow you to build a set of clubs that maximizes your strengths and minimizes your weaknesses. Virtually every respectable manufacturer has a system to help you find the club or clubs for you, and any good professional knows the importance of getting his or her players into the right equipment. Most manufacturers today have carts that allow you to choose from a variety of options. Choosing a club is not unlike selecting new lenses for glasses. Just as your eye doctor flips lens after lens and asks, "Better . . . worse," you should be that thorough in finding the right clubs.

You may have to make the transition from steel to graphite shafts, from forged blade to cavity-back investment cast, or from 200 CC head to 310 CC behemoth. Either way, the golf club doesn't know who's swinging it. It doesn't know how old you are, what sex you are, what shade you are. What it does know is whether the right person is swinging it.

Graphite A synthetic material used in shafts to decrease weight and thus improve swing speed. The process by which shafts are made provides shock absorption, lessening the stress on wrists, shoulders, and hands.

Investment cast Molds of clubheads are created, steel is poured into the mold, and the steel is cast in batches. Most clubs today are made in this form. Improvement in perimeter weighting is generally a tradeoff for less feel.

Perimeter weighting Distributing extra weight on the outsides of the clubhead to produce higher ball flight.

As you search for the right one for you, keep in mind where your game stands right now—whether it's progressed, regressed, or remained the same. The only thing worse than someone playing the wrong driver out of ignorance is someone playing the wrong driver out of pride. If you still crush the ball with a supple swing that hasn't changed in 30 years, give us your secret. But if you've noticed that you can't get that old steel telephone-pole shaft square at impact anymore, don't deny yourself the chance to keep playing solid golf. Find the right sticks and you won't drive your partners, spouse, neighbors, or clergy crazy. Here are some helpful hints in some important equipment categories.

Metalwoods

It certainly was hard to give up that persimmon driver, wasn't it? Well, for about nine holes anyway. The advent of the Gary Adams metalwood not only saved plenty of gorgeous trees but also altered the consciousness of golfers around the world. We grudgingly gave in to the newfangled and odd-looking weapon for one reason—it worked. Just like the rest of the golf nuts, we care about our scores and will do anything the United States Golf Association says we can to guarantee improvement. So we trade the "thwack" of persimmon for the "plink" of metal because it saves us strokes by giving us more distance and allowing us to hit more approach shots from the short grass.

As Adams was to the construction of the metalwood, so Ely Callaway is to the explosion of acceptance the clubs have enjoyed. Callaway's Big Bertha was the first club to be marketed by a business genius. His simple mantra, "We're committed to making a golf club that is pleasantly playable and demonstrably superior," was enough to make us all start with Bertha and work our way through her full-figured sisters, Great Big and Biggest Big, before working out with her brothers, Steelhead and Hawkeye. The franchise Callaway established set a pattern—what was once almost a grassroots business became a $2 billion global industry. Competitors were forced to work on tighter product cycles while looking for new materials and burgeoning markets, research and development departments had to build a club for today with another six on the drawing board, and marketing departments had to find a way to broadcast the message of better golf.

Part of the technology boom is the result of the end of the Cold War and the elimination of defense contracts. Plenty of aerospace engineers—experts in the ways and means of lift, drag, and trajectory—were looking for work. They brought that knowledge, a familiarity with metals and metal mixes, and a love of golf to the industry.

Ultimately, the equipment is "smarter," allowing us and our bad swings to think we're playing better golf. The reality is that we're getting better results from our bad swings. The new equipment provides more forgiveness than a cathedral of priests. The catch phrase we hear so often—"expanded sweet spot"—is the biggest falsehood in golf. The sweet spot in any golf club, regardless of the magnitude of the head, is as big as the head of a pin. It is nothing more than the precise center of the clubface. The hype is the result of an industry that is equal parts exact science and salable sound bite. When marketing types get the R&D people into a room, they say, "OK, give me the nut, the heart of the matter." The science people then look at them with disdain and try to marry physics, calculus, and metallurgy with snappy adjectives.

Compression The point at which a ball compresses at impact with the clubface. Most balls come in 80, 90, and 100 compressions. Balls with higher compression require greater force for full compression at impact. All three types will travel the same distance if struck with the appropriate force to maximize the energy transfer from club to ball.

This is where you come in. We benefit from this technology because these scientists are driven by the simple mandate of finding a way to make us play better. The care that goes into matching new metalwood heads with shafts is daunting to the lay person. But these new products allow us, especially as we age, to maximize limited mobility and slowed clubhead speed to give us acceptable, even surprising, distance off the tee and remarkable success from the fairway and especially from the rough. Although manufacturers introduce new materials and clubheads that go up and down in size and price, selecting a club, like selecting any other piece of equipment, boils down to appearance and performance—often in that order. How many times have you picked up a driver or fairway wood and were certain you wouldn't even try it? That first impression will lead you either to the practice tee or to another piece of equipment. With all the advancements in technology today, you can be sure that most clubs you'll investigate are well-crafted tools.

As you search for the right driver and fairway woods, one thing is certain—take the 1-, 2-, 3-, and perhaps even 4-irons out of your bags and find the right 7- and 9-woods for you. They are trustworthy, versatile, and easier to hit than those irons you had trouble hitting straight more than seven feet in the air 20 years ago.

Irons

Gary Player was discussing irons, more precisely, the difference between his irons today and the irons he used when he won the 1963 Masters: "I was puttering around in the basement when I stumbled on those irons and just for kicks, I took them out and hit some balls with them. I hit them like crap," he exclaimed. "There's no way I could go back to those after what we've been able to come up with today."

Thirty years ago, all that was available were steel forgings. You generally bought either Wilson or MacGregor and worked them so hard you wound up with a half-ball mark on the center of the clubface. You loved them unconditionally and treated them accordingly. Today, the irons market is like Baskin-Robbins—more choices, more flavors, more combinations, and even more money. Equipment manufacturers are asking consumers to make a sizable commitment when they buy a set of irons, so as we mentioned earlier, it's imperative that you be fitted properly when deciding on the right clubs.

Forging The process of creating a clubhead by heating a block of iron, shaping the clubhead, and then cooling, grinding and polishing to a high gloss. Forging is generally thought of as a process for making clubs for the better players, but technology has yielded some forgings for midhandicappers.

Offset A clubhead design feature in which the clubface sits slightly behind the hosel to help weaker players square the clubface at impact. Many iron sets feature progressive offset, in which the long irons feature maximum offset and the shorter irons have virtually none.

The advent of the perimeter-weighted, or game-improvement, irons opened the floodgates of opportunity for golfers. No longer were they required to try to hit a golf ball with something so small it was better suited to spreading butter on a roll. As these investment-cast irons made their mark on the industry, poor swings didn't cost players more than a stroke a hole; in many cases, players got away unscathed.

Over the years since Ping's Eye irons, companies have pushed the limits of clubhead size and perimeter weighting, moving the center of gravity down to help golfers get the ball up in the air with greater ease. Advancements in testing and research have unearthed a variety of new metals and metal mixes that allow clubs to become lighter, more durable, and better performing.

John Solheim, president of Ping, says he's not sure that the push for technology will ever stop. "I still can't believe the number of advancements that have been made since my dad began to make golf clubs," he says. "Then I take a look at what's gone on in the industry in the last five years and have no idea just how far we'll be able to go in the near, or distant, future." One thing is for sure, the merry-go-round won't stop.

A few years ago, the USGA announced that it could impose standards on the so-called trampoline effect, causing consternation and hand wringing throughout the golf industry, raising concerns that the concept of the clubface giving even just a little bit and in turn propelling the ball unfairly was going to ruin the game. The debate passed quietly, with the USGA essentially grandfathering the modern equipment as conforming.

But what has happened since is no surprise. Development has continued, and the movement toward bigger clubheads has been succeeded by a movement back to somewhat smaller heads and even a return to forgings. These forgings, however, could be hit by anyone, whether with a 2 or an 18 handicap. MacGregor and Tommy Armour brought out new forgings, and Callaway and Taylor Made created new metal mixes or steel versions of popular lines.

Again, what does it mean for the 50-plus crowd? It means more options in a variety of clubheads and materials and shafts that match performance and comfort.

Wedges

As we discussed in chapter 3, the short game is probably the most important part of any senior's game. You may not be hitting as many greens as you used to, so it's vital that you come up with a course of action for your game from 100 yards in.

Tommy Jacobs demonstrates the proper setup for a bladed wedge shot.

You, or most of your peers, no doubt carry three wedges. Some players even carry four. At the risk of sounding like an old crank, take the 60-degree model out of the bag if you're not going to practice with it constantly. That club requires hours of devotion or it will turn on you. We've all been through it— you haven't worked with it or used it at all in the round and on the 15th hole you're in some heavy cabbage and you think you're going to feather one next to the stick like Mickelson and Woods do. But you wind up putting a weak move on it and either go completely under the ball or blade it across the green onto the next tee.

A rule of thumb is to have about six degrees of separation from one wedge to the next. If your pitching wedge is 46 degrees, than a gap wedge of 52 degrees and a sand wedge of 58 will likely do the trick. When deciding on your wedge

With a 46-degree pitching wedge, carry a 52-degree gap wedge and a 58-degree sand wedge.

makeup, however, consider the course you play most often. If you've got slick, elevated greens that require a lot of spin, then put the 60-degree wedge in the bag. If you can bump and run, you may alter your set and go down as low as 56 degrees for your sand wedge.

Putters

The putter is either the most indispensable or the most despicable stick in your bag. You might have a blade that looks like a minigolf special from the '50s and hasn't been out of the bag since the day you bought it. On the other hand, your basement might have more castoffs than *Gilligan's Island.* Either way, this is by far the most subjective discussion in the equipment puzzle. The late Karsten Solheim, father of the Ping dynasty, created the prototype by which all subsequent models will be measured. His heel-toe weighting led to a crush of competitors, many of whom then followed the pioneers of Odyssey Golf, who created the face insert as a buffer for golfers who favored surlyn balls from tee to green but were looking for a way to get more feel on the putting green.

Heel-toe weighting Shifting weight of the clubhead out toward the toe and heel to expand the area on a club in which off-center hits will yield acceptable results.

Along with drivers, putters might be the most replaced club in the bag, which would explain a few things—why all manufacturers unveil model after model in hopes of catching lightning in a bottle; why every wingnut with a small machine shop, a level, and a design on a cocktail napkin thinks he's going to be the next Solheim; and why we just can't help ourselves from going into our friends' bags or garage-sale trash cans looking for The One. Finding the right putter is simply the transference of confidence, a conduit to helping you get the ball into the hole. Our advice to you is to find a putter that you feel at least somewhat comfortable with, consider the speed of the greens you normally play, select a putter with about two degrees of loft that reduces the initial skidding most putts generate, practice diligently, love it unequivocally, and don't tempt fate.

a

Tom Weiskopf *(a)* and Gary McCord *(b)* choose putters to match their putting styles.

b

Shoes

You may not believe that any other accoutrements fall under the equipment category, so humor us. If anything goes wrong with these items, your round will go south faster than a New Yorker who just saw the first snowflake of the year.

Let's consider shoes. Face it, you've been on your feet a long time. If you've never had a foot problem, knock on surlyn. But if you're sensitive to the beating your feet take on the golf course, heed some words to the wise: find a make and model that fit as if they were sewn on and get a couple pairs. Rotate the shoes to give the leather time to recover from perspiration and other moisture.

Also, consider your socks. If your socks are too thick, too thin, or too small, your preshot routine will include a profane thought that shouldn't have to be a concern.

Bags

If you carry your bag, the new shoulder-strap contraptions that make your bag look like a backpack may take a little getting used to, but they disperse the weight and don't put strain on just one shoulder. The new materials are lighter, which, if you don't carry your own bag, will make your caddie happy. Also, your bag may have a place for a cell phone, but for God's sake don't put one in there.

Hats and Sunglasses

We're not saying they have to be the annoying variety that about two people in a hundred can carry off with any panache, but as you know, the sun can do worlds of damage. Protect yourself and live to play another day.

Grips

If you suffer from arthritis, you'll be best served by getting oversized grips on your clubs. The increased size will allow you to get your hands around the club without having to squeeze too tightly. You will be able to rotate your hands more freely through the impact zone, giving you straighter shots.

An oversized grip can help your hands if you have arthritis.

The downside is that the bigger grips will cost you some yards. Your hands will be able to rotate through the ball, but they will not be able to rotate as quickly as they have in the past, which will cost you some distance.

You can add to the circumference of the grip end of the club in two ways—by adding layers of tape on the shaft before sliding new grips on or by getting specially made thicker grips, which you can order from most grip manufacturers.

Bend but Don't Break

We end our discussion of equipment by noting the importance of the shaft. Simply put, the shaft is the engine of the club. With the wrong shaft, you won't be able to hit a 90-yard-wide fairway or get it up in the air for longer than Orville and Wilbur Wright's first ill-fated endeavor. With the right shaft, you'll blow it over the pond with yards to spare and land it on the back of that butterfly you saw flitting down the middle of the fairway from the tee.

Torque The degree to which the shaft rotates during the swing.

Kickpoint The spot on a shaft at which it bends the most during the swing, dictating the flight of the ball. A low kickpoint will help get the ball airborne quicker and keep it in the air longer. Better players tend to favor higher kickpoints because they have no trouble getting the ball in the air.

As we age, we may feel the need to make the switch from steel to graphite for the comfort factor. Graphite's softer feel provides mild shock absorption and eases the stress on sore shoulders, elbows, and wrists. But whether you choose steel or graphite, don't be a hero.

Experiment with a variety of shafts to find the one that gives you the best marriage of distance and accuracy. "Stiff" is not an acceptable knee-jerk selection, for two reasons:

1. About 90 percent of the golfing population, regardless of age, should not be playing a stiff shaft.

2. The shaft is the least regulated piece of equipment. Consequently, one manufacturer's stiff shaft is another's regular, and another's regular is yet another's soft flex.

Loft The angle formed by the shaft and the bottom of the clubhead.

Lie The degree of lie is the club's angle for launching the ball. Short irons are more lofted than long irons.

Only you know precisely what sort of ball flight and trajectory you want to achieve, and only you will know which of the many shafts you've tried can give you that feedback. Again, try out a variety of clubhead and loft-and-lie options with a selection of shaft offerings to give yourself a shot at improving distance and accuracy.

With your fundamentals down pat, your equipment in your bag and ready to go, it's time to head to the practice range. Just as it is the way to get to Carnegie Hall, practice is also the way to improve your golf game.

7

Practicing for Perfection

The skills of golf are so precise and delicate that it's impossible for your brain to retain the sensory information for long. To sustain and improve your game, you must practice. But your practice will be effective only if it simulates the skills you use on the course. A session at a driving range in which you hit off an artificial surface may help you develop some aspects of your swing, but anything related to the grass hitting surface of the course, such as your stance and feel at impact, will be unrealistic.

Your practice routine should also involve pressure to perform. If you hit a bucket of balls in a relaxed manner, without demanding performance of yourself, how can you expect to respond to pressure on the course?

To add some pressure in practice, hit to a target and set goals for yourself, like trying to hit 10 out of 15 balls into a 15-yard circle. Be conscious of the time you're taking for each shot. It's unrealistic to hit many balls consecutively, so take a short break between shots just as you would on the course. Realign yourself and check your setup before you swing.

Shot Routine

Whether you're on the course or on the range, the best way to get in a consistent frame of mind for each shot is to undergo the same preshot routine. Every professional golfer has a routine that allows them to focus on the shot ahead. The repetition of a procedure eliminates your risk of error and helps you focus on the task ahead. If you address the ball with the same thoughts and ideas each time, your consistency certainly will improve.

Using a consistent shot routine helps your concentration.

Visualize the Shot

You should strive to learn the skill of standing behind your ball and imagining the shot you want to play. This skill, known as visualization, is widely endorsed by sport psychologists. Visualization can help you develop your sense of alignment, your timing, and your swing pattern. Developing this skill is not easy. Professional athletes from all sports spend hours practicing the drill. But even if you're not an expert, any image you can evoke will aid your sense of the shot you want to make. You may find it easier to close your eyes as you try to visualize yourself.

Choose Your Club

If you can find a system for choosing a club, you'll take the second-guessing out of your game. You need a method that eliminates the chance of simple errors.

Choosing the right club should become a natural part of your shot routine.

A routine for working out your yardage, considering your lie, assessing the wind, and imagining the shot will help you become more consistent. An established routine will give you confidence in tough conditions and keep your mental game in a steady state.

Get Into Your Stance

A good stance may not seem natural and may be uncomfortable at first. Professionals spend hours working on the angle of the spine and the bend in the legs. Because you bend your knees and your hips, you need some time before each shot to become comfortable and aligned. See the section on alignment in chapter 1 (page 12) for more tips.

Simplify Your Thinking

Once you step up to the ball, you don't want to confuse yourself with a multitude of thoughts about your swing. One or two thoughts will help keep you focused on specific skills and moves, and you can remember them by using one-word reminders, such as "slow," "low," or "inside." The easiest way to simplify your thoughts is to focus your eyes on a spot on the back of the ball, precisely where you want to hit it.

In summary, several key techniques will help you develop consistency:

- Stand behind the ball for a few seconds and visualize the shot you'd like to make.
- Develop a system for club selection. Learn to trust your instincts, make a decision, and stick with it.
- Develop a system for analyzing the wind, the conditions, your lie, and the surroundings.
- Design a system for getting into your stance, checking your posture, and checking your alignment.

- Develop consistency in the number of practice swings you take.
- Use just one or two swing thoughts as you address the ball.

Short-Game Problem Solving

Even with superb technique, your short game depends on "feel," your ability to judge and control the pace and direction of your shot. Consequently, practice is indispensable because feel is based on your frame of mind, previous experience, and familiarity with conditions and lies.

You can maximize your practice time to prepare yourself for the varying conditions in which you'll play. Practice your chipping, for example, from as many different lies as you can find. Don't limit your already limited practice time by simply hitting from perfect, short-grass lies. How many times do you hit a chip shot from a perfect lie? You should also practice your putting from various distances and slopes.

Bunker Play

A common mistake is not allowing the clubface to do the work. The club is designed to get the ball in the air in response to a normal swing. Many players unnecessarily try to muscle the clubface under the ball to get it airborne. On the other hand, you must swing solidly enough to keep the clubface square at impact, particularly if you're playing from rough or sand.

Putting

Your putting practice should be goal oriented. Try to sink a high percentage of short putts. Take time to line up each putt, just as you would on the course. Structure your practice time by hitting a set number of balls from each distance rather than randomly hitting balls without putting pressure on yourself.

Let the club loft you out of the sand.

Practice putting from a variety of situations.

PUTTING

Dave Stockton

Being a consistently good putter requires more than simply making a pure stroke. Mental outlook, green reading, setup, posture, touch, and effective practice all contribute to getting the ball into the hole. My 18-point checklist of putting principles gives you all the information you need to become deadly with the short stick.

Set Your Speed Limit

Most amateurs hit their putts too hard. I believe in rolling the ball just up to the hole instead of being too bold. On one of my favorite putting drills, I stick a tee 16 inches behind the hole. I putt from various distances, trying not to roll the ball past the tee. You'll be amazed at how many putts you sink—and you virtually eliminate those awful three-putts.

Never Hit the Back of the Cup

Try to make your putts without touching the back of the hole. Aim your read and your stroke at neatly rolling the ball over the front lip.

Know That Greens Change

The speed of greens varies throughout the day. Wet greens in the morning are slower than the dry, firm greens you'll play by the middle of the round. The smart putter will adjust speed and break accordingly.

Putt to the True Center of the Hole

Most golfers try to roll the ball into the center of the hole, based on a straight line running from the ball to the hole. But most putts have some break, so aim for the point that represents the center of the hole based on how the putt breaks.

Divide Putts Into Thirds

Study a longish putt from the low side and divide the length of the putt into three equal sections. During the middle third of the ball's roll, the contours begin to have their effect. Be extremely conscious of any breaks in the final third of the line because the ball is coming to a stop—that's where the break has the greatest effect.

Mentally divide a putt into three equal parts.

continued

Read From the Low Side

Over the years I've developed a system for reading the line that may help you. First, study the line from behind the ball to get an overview of the break. From there, go to the low side of the hole, midway along its length. You'll get a much better perspective of the overall break from below the hole than from above it.

Don't Judge by Someone Else's Putt

Most golfers try to "go to school" when one of their playing partners is putting first on a similar line. My advice is to make your own read. Why? You won't know how hard the other golfer hit the putt, so you don't know if yours will break the same (you may hit it slightly harder or softer). In addition, you can't tell whether the player has hit the putt solidly. Trust your own read and stroke. In most cases you'll come out ahead.

Don't trust another player's putt. Read the green yourself.

Position the Ball Slightly Farther Back

I recommend that you position the ball two to three inches inside your left heel. This lets you make a controlled swing back and allows you to bring it through with the same length and pace. If you play the ball too far forward, you will likely make a long backstroke, hit the ball, and then come to an abrupt stop.

Keep Hands Fairly High

Most golfers stand too far from the ball, forcing their hands too low. This causes right-handed players to miss putts left. If that's where you're struggling, stand a couple of inches closer to the ball and set your hands and wrists high. Doing this brings the clubshaft closer to vertical and places your eyes directly over the ball.

Stand Tall on Long Putts

Standing taller on putts of 30 feet or longer allows you to see the line a little better, encourages you stay in place, and helps you hit the putt solidly. You need to stay still and hit every putt squarely, of course, but this is especially important on longer putts. Assume a slightly taller posture, with your back more upright and your feet slightly closer together, than you do on the short ones.

Limit Practice Strokes

Most amateurs overrehearse their practice stroke rather than trusting their read and marrying their stroke to it. By the time you take three practice strokes, you've lost the mental picture of the speed and line. I know this sounds radical, but I recommend not taking any practice strokes. Once I factor in the speed and the line, I simply place the putter just in front of the ball, adjust my feet, replace the putter behind the ball, take one last look at the hole and go. Keep the feel of the putt fresh in your mind and stroke it decisively.

Always Play the Same Ball

Many amateurs change golf balls from one round to the next, or even during a round. This can hurt your putting—as well as your entire game. If you play Monday with a three-piece, balata-covered ball and Tuesday with a hard-covered two-piece ball, the second ball will feel different, roll a little farther, and, because it jumps off the putterface more, will even break a little less. Determine which ball is best for your total game and then stick with it. Also, make sure to practice with that model to maintain consistent feel.

continued

Widen Stance in the Wind

Playing in something more substantial than a gentle breeze makes it tough to stay perfectly still during the stroke. Widen your stance by a few inches when the wind is blowing hard. You'll remain steady back and through the ball and impart a true roll.

Widening your stance helps you stay balanced in strong winds.

Use Two Practice Balls, Tops

Most golfers practice their putting with at least three balls—some use a whole pile. Keep the extras in your bag. You only get one chance on the course, so don't hit putt after putt from the same spot on the practice green. It's OK to try a second from the same spot, but that's it. Using just two balls allows you to move around the green and try putts of a variety of lengths, speeds, and breaks. Using this routine better prepares you for the putts you'll have to make during a normal round.

Keep the Length of Stroke Even

You often hear that you should take a short backswing and then accelerate through the ball with a longer downswing. I disagree. Roll the ball smoothly to the hole instead of feeling as though you're "hitting" your putts. To do this, go back and through equally, with even pace throughout. You can develop this stroke by finding a putt that requires a certain stroke—say, 12 inches back and 12 inches through. Set a tee in the ground 12 inches behind the ball and another tee 12 inches in front of the ball. Then watch the putter blade to see whether you maintain the proper stroke rhythm while hitting the tees.

Always Keep Putterhead Low

I believe the best stroke keeps the putterhead low, with a dominant left hand (for right-handed players). If you raise the putterhead too far off the ground on the backswing and especially on the downstroke, you're less likely to make the solid, square impact necessary for a true roll. A helpful practice drill is to make your stroke and then rest the putterhead on the ground at the completion of the follow-through. If you have more than an inch between the sole and the ground on a midrange putt, extend the back of your left hand out even more beyond impact to keep the putterhead low.

Increase Loft if Putts Are Bumpy

Good putters produce a smooth roll, whereas poor putters seem to bounce the ball to the hole. The bouncing roll is often the result of having the hands and clubshaft too far ahead of the clubface at impact. This placement delofts the clubface. Almost all putters have some loft, so at address place your hands even with the ball. At this point, you can use a slight "forward press" to start the stroke and still have enough loft at impact to roll the ball smoothly.

End With Short Ones

Always spend several minutes on the practice green before you tee off and finish every putting warm-up by holing several two- and three-footers. You'll need to make a few of these during every round—making them could be the difference between a fair round and a good one. Sinking several putts also provides extra confidence as you go to the first tee.

This chapter has emphasized some ways to develop consistency in your game. It all starts with quality practice, but on-course tricks can help too. As Dave Stockton has shown you, good putting is the result of developing routines that make you think yet also allow you to play with natural flair.

Now that you have developed your game, let's give your body the best chance of providing you with energy and power—both mental and physical. In the next chapter, we'll show you how to eat well, on and off the course.

chapter

8

Fueling Up

To be effective on the course, you need enough energy to maintain your strength and stamina. Unfortunately, a diet that will magically elevate your game doesn't exist. Still, it's important that you eat a well-balanced diet to replace the energy that you're expending and promote general health. Foods are composed of nutrients. The ideal diet for your health provides 60 percent of calories from carbohydrates, 10 percent of calories from protein, and 30 percent of calories from fat.

Assuming you use more energy playing golf than you do during your usual daily schedule, you simply need to supplement your eating with some carbohydrate-based foods or snacks before and during the round. Having said that, you don't want excess food in your stomach when you tee off, so you should avoid eating a large meal before you play.

Some snack foods supply 60 percent or more of their calories from fat. Your body can convert fat calories to energy, though not as effectively as it can those derived from carbohydrate foods. In general, Americans eat too much food but too few carbohydrates.

Carbohydrates are the food nutrient that provides energy your body can store and use easily. Fat not used by your body often remains in your body as fat.

The ideal time to eat your preround meal is a couple of hours before you tee it up. Your body has enough time to digest the food, so you can step onto the course feeling comfortable. Once you start playing, small snacks will help you avoid hunger pains and maintain a high energy level.

The most effective form of energy is found in foods such as vegetables, fruit, and grain products. Containing small amounts of fat, these foods are made up of nutrients that your body can easily convert into energy. For a snack during a round, you might try the clubhouse snack bar. Few of the many choices available there, however, are likely to be healthy ones.

You may have seen the large bowl of fruit available for professionals on tee boxes on professional tours. Gary Player started eating fruit on the course well before other players, and most of his peers now realize the value of fruit ahead of other snacks.

Fruit is a great choice for snacking.

Most packaged foods have a food label that tells you how many of the total calories in the product are derived from fat. Using those figures, you can work out the fat percentage of the food. If it's a high percentage (more than 30 percent), healthier options are usually available.

High-Carbohydrate Snacks

vegetables

fruits

bread

bagels

pretzels

graham crackers or saltines

FOOD FOR THOUGHT

Jay Sigel

On competition days, I'm very aware of how I eat. If I tee off early, I'll try to eat a lot of carbohydrates because I won't really have any lunch. For breakfast I might have some pancakes and some fruit. Then I keep eating snacks throughout the round. It's amazing that you can sometimes feel your energy just leaving your body. I might have one banana before I tee off, then another two during a round. I drink a lot of fluids, mostly water, but I occasionally drink Gatorade. You can become dehydrated without knowing it. Off the course I watch out for fatty foods. For dinner, I like pasta, fish, or chicken courses. My wife and I eat lots of vegetables and fruit.

Protein: How Much

Most Americans eat twice as much protein as they need, and the body converts the excess protein to fat. Protein, however, does perform many important functions for your body. Your bones and muscles, for example, are composed of a variety of proteins.

Protein cannot be stored in your body, so you need to consume foods with protein regularly. Protein is highly concentrated in animal product foods such as meat, poultry, dairy products, fish, and eggs.

Because your requirements for protein decrease with age, you may want to evaluate your diet periodically. A registered dietitian can help you determine how much protein you're consuming. Don't be surprised if he or she recommends supplementing carbohydrate foods for some of the fish and meat you may be typically eating.

High-Protein Foods

fish

chicken

lean beef

peanut butter

soy products

turkey

Hydration:
The Importance of Fluids

Liquids help regulate the temperature of the body and flush out toxic wastes. Few golfers realize the importance of staying hydrated during a round. Studies have shown that dehydration is a major cause of fatigue and illness. Golfers are at a high risk, particularly in hot weather. Be aware that thirst is a poor indicator of the fluid needs of your body. If you don't drink until you're thirsty, you've waited far too long.

Drink water to stay hydrated.

A good rule of thumb is to drink a cup of liquid every 15 minutes. Many professionals, out of habit, take a drink on every tee.

During a round, try to avoid carbonated drinks such as sodas and even carbonated water. It's a hotly debated question as to whether energy and sports drinks are more effective than water, but both are healthy alternatives. Just remember that sports drinks often have many calories.

As you can see, eating well requires no magic. The truth is that nothing beats a balanced diet with plenty of fruits and vegetables.

Changing your eating habits isn't easy, but you'll reap the long-term rewards from making small changes, such as eating fruit instead of potato chips or drinking water instead of soda. It may not improve your game, but good health will keep you on the course for many years to come.

Most important, stay hydrated on the course. Carry a bottle of juice or water, and regardless of the weather, drink regularly.

GOLF AND NUTRITION

Chris Rosenbloom, PhD, RD
Nutrition Consultant to Georgia Tech Athletic Association

Golfers often talk about course management but rarely discuss diet management. As we age, our need for calories, nutrients, and fluids changes. If you're aware of these changes, you can take steps to maximize your nutrition and performance.

Our energy and calorie needs decline with age. If you continue to consume the same amount of food you did when you were young, you'll likely put on weight. This weight creep sets the stage for high blood pressure, heart disease, and diabetes.

By taking a few key steps, you can improve the way you feel on the course. First, you should get your blood sugar level on track for the day—and keep it at a good level. Second, stay hydrated. The older we get, the more vulnerable we are to dehydration. Decreasing kidney function, a reduced sense of thirst, and lower amounts of total body water all contribute to dehydration. The good news is that it's 100 percent preventable.

Here are my suggestions.

Start Your Day With Style

Regardless of your tee time, don't leave home without eating breakfast. Bagels, cereal with skim milk, fruit, and fruit juices are the best foods for energy.

Think Fluids

Regardless of the weather, drink two cups of water or juice before you tee off and take a gulp of water every 10 to 15 minutes. You should take a water bottle with you and fill it at every opportunity.

Sports drinks are good choices for replacing water, nutrients, and electrolytes, but avoid caffeinated drinks because they can contribute to dehydration.

Snack Sensibly

Don't sabotage your exercise on the course with high-fat foods from the snack bar. Fruit, bagels, pretzels, grilled chicken, and turkey are great snack foods.

Reprinted from *Senior Golfer* magazine.

chapter

9

Keeping the Fun in the Game

Your enjoyment of the game will depend on your attitude toward why you play. If you're highly competitive, for example, and competition is the reason you play, then your satisfaction will depend on your ability to win. However, we hope that you take a more holistic approach, regardless of your playing level. Most amateurs see the game as a combination of experiences—the challenge of mind and body, the companionship of friends, and the benefits of some exercise.

As long as you keep those elements in perspective on the course, you can deeply enjoy the game. If you become absorbed by one goal, you're likely to be disappointed.

Playing well is important to everyone, of course, but we sometimes fail to reach our personal standards. Other goals, however, we can reach consistently. If health and fitness are your primary reasons for playing, for example, you simply will see golf as an interrupted walk. Performance becomes less important to your overall enjoyment.

In terms of playing to the best of your ability, it's often difficult to accept the stupid mistakes you make on the course. But golf is a highly technical sport that requires precision and practice. It's a game of inches, and it's unlikely that you'll ever produce the overall accuracy you want.

Sometimes you'll get a good bounce and have some luck, and other times you won't. The reality is that unless you play

Senior PGA Tour player George Archer.

often and have considerable talent for the game, it's unlikely that you will play your best golf very often. Even Senior PGA Tour player George Archer accepts that some days good luck is not on your side. "There are times when you hit a perfect drive and it lands in a divot," Archer says. "Other times you mis-hit the ball and it ends up perfectly. How can you explain it?"

Many amateurs have expectations beyond their talents or the time and practice they put into improving. Their reactions to bad shots often create an uneasy feeling on the course and can cause slow play. Decide what you want to get out of the game and be realistic about what you can achieve.

You Against Yourself and the Course

Without you realizing it, your playing partners may be distracting you from your game. Their personalities may be affecting your performance and even your enjoyment. You may find it beneficial to shift your interest toward the challenge of the course, playing against yourself. By concentrating on your own game, you can enjoy the company of the group without worrying about their scores or games.

Patience

There's no doubt about it—golf requires patience. No matter how hard you try, it's sometimes impossible to hit the ball straight or make a decent score. Playing poorly can be frustrating, but if you allow resentment to build, your performance will only worsen. Serious doubts may creep into your game. Don't waste your mental energy by cursing shots you have already made. Once the ball leaves the clubface, there's not much you can do to change its direction. Take each hole as a different challenge and don't dwell on the past—keep thinking ahead.

Mechanical Minds

In a game that's overrun by swing doctors offering swing tips, it's easy to become obsessed with mechanics. Every now and then, you must just rely on your instincts and simply hit the ball without thinking about it. You may find that playing instinctively helps you relax and changes some habits that aren't working for you.

Analyzing Your Game

At the end of a round, how do you assess your game? Many players go from week to week without solid information about their games. They invest time improving their overall play without focusing on the skills that could most rapidly improve their scores. You may find the game more enjoyable if you work on specific skills based on your strengths and weaknesses. Try analyzing the details of your game—which clubs you hit, what success you had with putting, where and how you made mistakes.

A chart like the one shown here can help you analyze your play on every hole.

Building Your Confidence

Everyone has quirks or superstitions. For example, Larry Nelson often uses several putters during a tournament. "It's not the actual putter that matters," he says. "I'm just looking for something to build my confidence around every day."

By constantly searching for a new putter, Nelson has found a successful way of ignoring doubts and concerns about other parts of his game. The process of selecting putters also means he does a lot of putting practice—hundreds of putts for each new putter! Nelson's methods may not work for you, but you can learn much from his thinking.

The message here is that you should seek ways to arrive at the course ready to play. The great players find ways to build

PLAY ANALYSIS

Hole	Par	Score	Tee shot	Approach and short game	Putts	Notes
1						
2						
3						
4						
5						
6						
7						
8						
9						
10						
11						
12						
13						
14						
15						
16						
17						
18						

Larry Nelson changes putters to build his confidence.

confidence, even when their games go south. They know that confidence comes primarily from hard work, but they also use tricks to give their confidence a chance to improve.

Trying New Skills

If you want to keep improving as you age, you'll need to find new skills to compensate for the physical changes in your body. The secret is not expecting too much too soon. A swing adjustment can take months before it becomes effective, so if you're convinced the change will be positive, stick with it—however frustrating that may be. If you change your game every time you play, you can't expect to improve. Find a plan and go with it. Reassess the situation no more often than once a month.

Taking a Break

You may play so much that you simply need a break. If you're not happy with your game, you may have slipped into some bad habits. A break from the game is sometimes the most effective way to start a fresh approach. Spend a weekend fishing!

Smelling the Flowers

How much are you aware of the physical environment of the course? Can you name the trees and birds on the course? Taking your mind away from your game during a round may be useful. You may not have the mental concentration or fitness you once had, so thinking about something else between shots may help you relax.

It's easy to lose sight of why we're out on the course. You'll see people on every course who don't look as if they're enjoying themselves. Most of our expectations are usually well beyond our abilities, so it's easy to become frustrated on the course!

In this chapter, we've asked you to assess your reasons and motivations for playing. You may improve your game by taking a fresh mental approach. Think about how you react to a bad shot or bad luck, and learn to enjoy the game. At the very least, enjoy the health benefits and exercise.

Index

The italicized *f* following page numbers refers to photographs or figures that illustrate the topic.

About the Authors

David Chmiel

David Chmiel is editor in chief of *Senior Golfer*, a national publication geared toward golfers 50 and over. Previously, he served as managing editor of *Golf Pro*, where he wrote news features and opinion pieces and edited other writers' contributions to the magazine. A graduate of Temple University, David holds a BA in English. He is a member of the Golf Writers Association of America, the Metropolitan Golf Writers Association, and the International Network of Golf. He was awarded the Neal Award by the American Business Press for his story, "Cash and Carry," which appeared in *Golf Pro* magazine in September 1993. In his leisure time, David enjoys playing golf and basketball, reading, music, and home repair. He lives in Maplewood, New Jersey.

Kevin Morris

Dr. Kevin Morris is the managing editor of features at *Senior Golfer* magazine. He has a doctorate in physical education and sports and is a visiting lecturer at Boston University. He is a member of the Metropolitan Golf Writers Association and the American College of Sports Medicine. A resident of Bronxville, New York, Kevin enjoys playing golf and visiting his family in New Zealand.

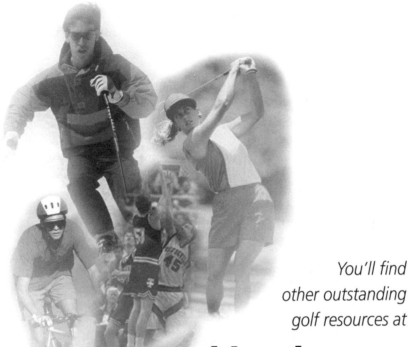

You'll find
other outstanding
golf resources at

www.humankinetics.com

In the U.S. call

1-800-747-4457

Australia 08 8277 1555
Canada 800-465-7301
Europe .... +44 (0) 113 278 1708
New Zealand 09-309-1890

HUMAN KINETICS
The Premier Publisher for Sports and Fitness
P.O. Box 5076 • Champaign, IL 61825-5076 USA